I know
what
you are

D1078480

I know what you are

TAYLOR EDISON
AND JANE SMITH

The true story of
a lonely little girl
abused by those
she trusted most

HARPER
element

Certain details in this story, including names, places and dates, have been changed to protect the family's privacy.

HarperElement
An imprint of HarperCollins*Publishers*
1 London Bridge Street
London SE1 9GF

www.harpercollins.co.uk

First published by HarperElement 2017

1 3 5 7 9 10 8 6 4 2

© Taylor Edison and Jane Smith 2017

Taylor Edison and Jane Smith assert the moral right to be identified as the authors of this work

A catalogue record of this book is available from the British Library

PB ISBN 978-0-00-814802-7
EB ISBN 978-0-00-815738-8

Printed and bound in Great Britain by
Clays Ltd, St Ives plc

All rights reserved. No part of this publication may be reproduced, stored in a retrieval system, or transmitted, in any form or by any means, electronic, mechanical, photocopying, recording or otherwise, without the prior written permission of the publishers.

MIX
Paper from
responsible sources

FSC
www.fsc.org   **FSC˚ C007454**

FSC™ is a non-profit international organisation established to promote the responsible management of the world's forests. Products carrying the FSC label are independently certified to assure consumers that they come from forests that are managed to meet the social, economic and ecological needs of present or future generations, and other controlled sources.

Find out more about HarperCollins and the environment at
www.harpercollins.co.uk/green

362·1968

Preface

I used to feel angry with my mum because she didn't intervene in what was going on when I was a child. But I realise that she's got problems of her own and I just feel sorry for her now. What made me look at things differently was becoming a mum myself: I try really hard to do what's best for my child – it's just a natural instinct; so I think my mum must have been trying hard too.

I would have liked to have told my story without mentioning Mum at all, and especially without saying anything negative about her. But because most of it deals with abuse that occurred during my childhood, that would have made it seem as though she wasn't there while I was growing up. And that isn't true. So I'm just going to tell it the way it happened.

There are lots of reasons why people fall victim to abusers. In my case, it was partly because I have a type of autism called Asperger syndrome, which means that I have 'significant difficulties in social interaction and non-verbal communication'. In other words, if someone tells me they're my friend, for example, I believe them, even though the way they're treating me is anything but friendly.

Friends have been a significant factor in my life – because I desperately wanted them as a child, because I didn't know how to make them, and because my 'social interaction and non-verbal communication' problems meant that, for a long time, I wasn't able to distinguish between my friends and my enemies.

I can't change what happened to me from the age of 11. I know that some of it will continue to have an effect on me for the rest of my life. But I do try really hard to remember that I am *not* the bad person I believed I was when I was a little girl.

What's crucially important when you have experienced abuse is to try not to define yourself in terms of 'bad things happened to me as a child because I was a bad child'. That's why I want to tell my story, because I hope it will help other people to realise that what is *done* to you isn't what you *are*.

Chapter 1

I was two years old when Mum and I moved into the flat that quickly became a doss-house for an assortment of her weed-smoking friends. I didn't have a bedroom of my own in that flat; my bed was wherever I happened to fall asleep each night, which was usually on the sofa or floor in the living room. Fortunately, Mum's friends were nice to me and there was always someone who was willing (and able) to feed me when I was hungry or put me in the bath when I needed a wash. So I was perfectly happy, as far as I remember. Until I started school.

Because I had assumed – as children tend to do without even thinking about it – that what happened in my own home was 'normal', school came as a complete shock to me, for many reasons. As I hadn't really mixed with other kids before I started school,

I didn't know how to make friends or even how to play with other children. And I wasn't used to being shouted at the way my teacher shouted at me on my very first day when I didn't do something she had told me to do.

I wasn't being deliberately disobedient or naughty. I just didn't understand what she meant. I was used to being given simple directions by my mum and her friends – 'Stop it', 'Eat it', 'Go to sleep' – and I was bewildered by the teacher's collective instructions to the class, which became even more incomprehensible to me when she said things like, 'Unfortunately, we won't be able to go outside at playtime today as it's still raining cats and dogs.'

It didn't matter how hard I tried to understand what I was supposed to be doing, I invariably seemed to get it wrong. So I was always either already in trouble or feeling sick with apprehension, which meant that school was pretty much ruined for me right from the start.

Another thing I hated about school was that it meant being away from my mum, which was something I wasn't used to, although that was true for most of the other children too, I suppose. I don't have many specific memories of my mum when I was a young child, but I know she was almost always there – in body, if not in spirit – and that I never spent a single night away from home when I was a little girl. In fact, Mum and I had a very close relationship at that time, and even though it might have been odd and dysfunctional in some ways, at least it was familiar and comprehensible to me. I could tell when she was angry, for example, and I usually knew why; while she knew how to talk to me in a way that I could understand and that didn't trigger a meltdown in my weirdly wired brain.

But I didn't understand my teachers, and because the lack of comprehension was mutual, they would often back me into a corner, literally as well as figuratively, so that I felt trapped and panicked. As a result, it wasn't long before a hostile relationship began to develop between me and my teachers, which, far from trying to rectify, Mum sometimes seemed actively to encourage. After being happy to let other people take care of me since we'd moved into the flat that was always full of her drunk and drug-addicted friends, I think the time when I started school coincided with a phase when she wanted it to be just her and me against the rest of the world. So maybe she resented the influence she thought my teachers would have on me, or perhaps it simply felt as though she was getting her own back on all the teachers she used to tell me about who she hadn't liked when she was a child.

I didn't want to be in conflict with anyone though, and as well as trying – and usually failing – not to annoy my teachers, I longed to be like the other kids, who seemed to be able to follow instructions that, to me, seemed impossibly complicated and indecipherable. I hadn't been at school for very long before I realised that there must be something wrong with me, which I assumed was the fact that I was 'retarded', as Mum often told me I was. And that made me even more anxious to learn to behave the way the other kids did, because I really didn't want to have to go to a 'special school' like the one Mum described to me, where they sent children who weren't 'normal'.

Even when I was diagnosed as having Asperger syndrome, which was something that apparently couldn't be 'cured', I think Mum still preferred to believe I was 'retarded', because that was something she thought I *could* recover from, if only I tried hard enough. Perhaps her intentions were basically good, in that she was hoping to push me towards normality by refusing to accept that I had a problem. Or maybe she was just hoping that, whatever the problem was, it would go away if we ignored it.

It didn't go away though. It just got worse, until, eventually, I was so confused, lonely and unhappy I would have done almost anything to feel that my mother loved and approved of me, or that I had just one real friend. And then that became the real problem, because being desperate for affection puts any child in a potentially dangerous situation, particularly a child like me, who was already vulnerable for other reasons.

It wasn't until I started school that I realised I didn't have a dad. Even then, it didn't seem like a huge deal, because I wasn't the only child whose dad wasn't around, although I think most of the others at least knew who their fathers were, whereas I didn't know anything about mine.

I've never met my dad and Mum has never talked about him, except to say that he left before I was born. Perhaps he didn't even know Mum was pregnant and so has no idea that he has been a father for the last 21 years. I sometimes wonder if things might have been better – for Mum *and* for me – if he had stuck around while I was growing up. I don't *wish* he had though, because he might have made things worse, especially if he was an alcoholic or a drug addict, like most of Mum's friends when I was a child. And, in my experience, getting the thing you wish for doesn't always turn out well.

Mum was living with someone else when she met my dad, and when she got pregnant he threw her out. So she moved in with her mum, and that's where I lived, too, from the time I was born until I was two years old.

Grandma was in her forties when she had Mum, and Mum was in her thirties when she had me. So Grandma was well over 70 by the time I was born, and was already suffering from whatever it was that killed her when I was five. I don't have any clear memories of my grandma. I don't think she played a very active role in the first few years of my life, because she was ill and because she and my mum didn't get on.

My only other close relative is Mum's cousin, Cora, who lived in a flat in the house next door to Grandma. Cora suffers from depression and often finds life a bit of a struggle. But she has always worked hard and has done quite well for herself – which was fortunate for Mum and me, because when Grandma threw Mum out, Cora let us live in another property she owned. I don't know where we would have gone if she hadn't helped us, because, unlike her cousin, Mum has never worked or owned anything.

We are the sort of family that doesn't talk about anything important. So I don't know what caused

Cora's mental-health problems, or why Grandma and Mum didn't get on, or why Mum was only able to deal with life at all when she was separated from reality by a haze of cannabis smoke. I do know that I was very difficult as a child. At least, that's what Mum always told me, and I have to assume it was true, because I was certainly 'difficult' a few years later. Even so, maybe it's something no child needs to be told, and certainly not repeatedly.

Growing up knowing that your mum is having a horrible time and hating every minute of her life is bad enough. Believing that it's all your fault can provide the momentum that keeps the vicious circle of stress and bad behaviour spinning. It didn't do much for my confidence or self-esteem either. What made it even worse was the fact that I can't read or interpret people's expressions and body language, which meant that, as a child, I simply accepted whatever I was told as fact. Taking everything literally can be confusing at any age, but particularly when you're a child trying to make sense of the world for the first time. So, as far as I was concerned, I *was* difficult and I was the sole cause of all Mum's frustrations, disappointments and anger. Otherwise, why would she have said I was?

* * *

Fortunately, after we moved out of Grandma's place and into Cora's other property, Mum made friends with a couple who lived in the flat downstairs and who enjoyed smoking weed almost as much as she did. The fortunate bit about it, for me, was the fact that they were happy to help her look after me. Someone who's pretty much stoned from shortly after her first cup of tea in the morning until she falls asleep at night does need *some* help taking care of a two-year-old child and, as it turned out, three pot-heads are better than one.

It wasn't long, though, before our flat had become a doss-house for numerous alcoholics, drug addicts and petty thieves. Having grown up in the 1960s and 1970s, Mum saw it as a sort of hippy commune, which, to her, was something positive. And it did have some positive aspects. But, even taking those into account, it wasn't a good environment for any child to grow up in, for lots of reasons.

Despite all the pitfalls and potential dangers, however, everyone was very nice to me and I was never abused or neglected while we lived there. Mum's friends might have been doing irrevocable damage to their own lives and mental health, but they were mostly more 'peace and love' than intent on kicking anyone's head in. So the atmosphere was usually quite relaxed and there was rarely any aggression – as there might easily have been with so many dysfunctional, ultimately self-destructive people living together in one room.

Having so many people dossing in the flat also meant that on the many occasions when Mum was too stoned to remember she even *had* a child, there was always someone who was clear-headed enough to be able to put me in the bath, get me a drink from the kitchen or take me out to McDonald's and buy me something to eat.

From the little I know about Mum's life before I was old enough to understand things myself, I think she was already quite heavily involved with drugs by the time I was born. She told me once that she stopped taking speed and ecstasy when she was pregnant, but that she still smoked a lot of weed. I remembered that recently, when I read something about smoking weed in pregnancy possibly having a negative effect on the development of the baby's brain and behaviour. I wonder what my life would be like now if I hadn't grown up believing that all my behavioural problems – and the frustration and distress they caused Mum – were my fault.

After we had been living at the flat for a while, some of Mum's friends started getting addicted to more serious drugs. I think it was because they were stealing to feed their habit and then got involved with petty criminals and drug dealers who had their own, financial, reasons for wanting to get them hooked on something harder than cannabis. I think that was why things began to take a darker turn at the flat. There was certainly a period Mum has never wanted to talk about. Although I was very young, I have a clear memory that must have been during that time of climbing up on to a man's knee and not being able to wake him up, then hearing Mum telling someone later that he had overdosed and was actually dead in the chair.

I was too young to understand any of it. So I am not consciously aware of any bad memories associated with that time. Maybe I wasn't always happy there though, because I tried to run away on at least one occasion. Apparently, I managed to drag my bicycle down the steps at the front of the house and on to the pavement without anyone noticing. Then I cycled to the corner shop and sat with the shopkeeper for a whole hour before he realised no one was coming for me and took me home.

The flat had one bedroom and a high-ceilinged living room that was always full of people sleeping, smoking and drinking. Everyone made a mess and no one ever cleaned it up, except to wash a plate or a cup on a strictly as-needed basis or to scrape up the occasional congealed mess of vomit after someone had been sick in a corner of the room. I didn't have a bed of my own, so I slept in a drawer until I got too big for it, then in Mum's bed or on the sofa in the living room, or wherever else I happened to be when I fell asleep amongst all the prostrate bodies.

I thought everyone lived like we did and just accepted it all as normal. I didn't know anything else, and as none of Mum's friends had children of their own, I didn't have any other child's life to compare with mine. In fact, I had just one friend at that time, a little girl called Judy, who lived a few doors away and was probably 11 years old when I was four. But as her mum was a serious drug addict, my life seemed pretty good compared with hers. Despite never having been looked after in any practical or emotional way herself, Judy took care of her little sister almost from the day she was born, and often fed and played with me too.

Eventually, when I was five, Cora got fed up with her flat being used as a doss-house and told Mum she would have to find somewhere else to live. And as Mum had recently started seeing a guy called Dan, we moved in with him.

The fact that Dan was an alcoholic would have been enough to make him an unsuitable stepfather for any child. But he took the place of the dad I didn't have and was always good to me. (I always called him my stepdad, although he didn't actually marry my mum.) Despite his drinking, he was still managing to hold down a job – as a sort of cowboy builder – when we moved in with him. So at least someone was bringing money into the household.

At Dan's house, I had my own bed at last, in the basement. More importantly though, I had stepsiblings. Dan had two daughters, aged seven and eight, and three sons in their teens, although only the two younger ones ever stayed overnight. Even with my problems interpreting social interaction, it was clear to me right from the start that Dan's children didn't like me. Looking back on it now, I suppose they had enough troubles of their own, having to cope with being dumped at irregular intervals by one alcoholic parent on the other. So I must have seemed like a cuckoo in their already overcrowded nest. But I was too young to understand that at the time. I thought it was for purely personal reasons that they would push me down the stairs or wrap me in a blanket and sit on my head until I became hysterical with breathless panic. They may have disliked me too, of course.

But, whatever their reasons for bullying and teasing me, I know I was easy prey.

When Dan was at work, Mum usually went out as well, leaving me in the house to be looked after by the other kids, who, when they weren't tormenting me, took me shoplifting. I imagine all children want to be liked; I was the sort of child who wanted it desperately. And, like any other desperate need, that made me vulnerable. Add to that the fact that I was gullible, naive and totally lacking in social awareness, and you can understand why I was like putty in their hands.

When the adults were out and my stepbrothers took me into town, it was my job to distract the shop assistant in whichever shop they chose as their target for the day. Having been well instructed and rehearsed, I would peer over the counter and say, in my sweetest, most innocent-sounding voice, 'Excuse me. Can you help me, please? I want to buy a present for my mum.' Then, while the shop assistant's attention was focused on helping *me*, my stepbrothers would be helping themselves to whatever they wanted off the shelves. Surprisingly, perhaps, we didn't ever get caught, although our success might have been due to the fact that we were taking advantage of the kindness of decent people who didn't expect to be conned by a five-year-old child, rather than to any great skill on our behalf.

My stepsiblings were supposed to live most of the time with their mum, but she often dropped them off at their dad's house when she got tired of looking after them or had better things to do. Dan's eldest son used to visit us sometimes too. I always liked it when he came because, unlike his siblings, he was really nice to me and would spend ages styling my hair and putting varnish on my fingernails. Then, one day, his dad found out he was gay and beat the crap out of him, and he didn't ever come again.

The only other time I remember my stepdad being as angry as he was that day was when I was six and one of my stepbrothers tried to touch me 'down there'. Mum thought it was funny – the only time she ever really got angry was when something or someone threatened to disrupt her own life. But my stepdad went ballistic. The next thing I remember is sitting in the car outside a house with a white fence, watching anxiously while he and a woman screamed and shouted at each other. I thought it was all my fault, for some reason I didn't understand. So, although I was frightened by the row he was having with the woman – who turned out to be his ex-wife

– I was a bit relieved too, because Dan seemed to be blaming *her* for what happened.

Although I think, in that instance at least, both parents were probably equally to blame, Dan's ex-wife did often push her luck with him in a way that I don't think my mum would have dared to do. For example, she would sometimes drop the four younger children at our house to stay with their dad for the weekend, then turn off her phone and go missing for a couple of weeks. When I think about it now, it's hardly surprising my stepsiblings all had behavioural problems: no child should be treated like the prize in a game of pass the parcel that neither of their parents wants to win.

After living in Dan's place for a while, we all moved into a larger house. I think Dan might have had some connection with the landlord, maybe through his work as a builder, because the house was very old and in such a terrible state that it probably shouldn't have been rented out at all. It was demolished not long after we lived there, torn down along with a lot of other houses in the area to make way for brand new homes. So I suspect its fate had already been sealed before we moved in.

One of the worst things about the house we lived in with Dan was the bathroom. It was downstairs, next to the kitchen, and its floor was made of bare concrete that stopped short of the bath, so that the legs of the bathtub were resting on soil. Every time it rained, water seeped up through the ground and flooded the room with evil-smelling mud. It would spread to the kitchen too, where the dank spaces under the cupboards were home to an assortment of snails, slugs and woodlice.

It was odd that Mum didn't seem to mind living like that, particularly in view of the fact that later, when we moved again, she became obsessed with keeping our house clean. Perhaps it was just that a flooded bathroom was the least of her worries, compared to having been landed with four children she didn't want in addition to the one she already had.

I don't have many specific memories of Mum either being there or not being there during that period of my childhood. I know she was still smoking a lot of weed, so perhaps she was there more than I remember, but in the background somewhere, unnoticed in the noisy chaos of all the lives being lived around her. What I *do* remember is that Mum didn't cook and I was always hungry. She didn't enjoy cooking, so she simply refused to do it, even when Dan was out at work all day and there were five children who needed to be fed. When Dan *was* at home, he made just two things: porridge and spaghetti Bolognese. But mostly we ate takeaways.

After we had lived for a few months in the house with the muddy bathroom floor, Dan's alcoholism began to get really bad. Even when he was working, he must have struggled to pay the bills for all of us, plus whatever he spent on alcohol for himself and weed for him and Mum. Things got even tighter when he started turning up at building jobs drunk at 9 o'clock in the morning and getting sent home. Eventually, when he stopped working altogether, he would sit around in the park all day, drinking with the other alcoholics who went there to while away their jobless hours.

Then, one day, Dan's kids simply disappeared. I didn't know what had happened to them: one minute they were there, teasing or tolerating me; the next minute they had gone. It wasn't until much later that I found out they had been taken into care. Apparently, after moving on from using me as a decoy for their shoplifting exploits, the two boys had begun to get involved in more serious forms of petty crime. Then one of my stepsisters got an infection and was taken to hospital, where she was flagged up as 'at risk'.

There were lots of things that didn't make sense to me at that time – and there are many things that still don't. But although I might not have understood what being taken into care meant, it would have been better if someone had given me some kind of explanation rather than none at all. As it was, the sudden, mystifying disappearance of my four stepsiblings was just one more of the many incidents that occurred during my young life that made me feel anxious and insecure.

Fortunately – perhaps – I always managed to escape the attention of social services as a child. I think there were two reasons for that: because Mum always kept me away from hospitals and because I was always clean and reasonably well dressed in clothes that were shabby but appropriate for my age. The reason for the first explanation was that Mum had been in care herself as a child and didn't want me to experience whatever it was that had happened to *her*. The reason for the second seems to have been that as long as I wasn't dirty, obviously malnourished or underweight, the social workers who never quite became involved in my childhood assumed I was being adequately looked after.

You can't really blame the social workers for being fooled and for just scratching the surface. They must have seen lots of children who were more obviously at risk and more in need of their attention. And I think, particularly as I got older, they sympathised with Mum for having to cope with such an exhaustingly difficult child.

Eventually, and inevitably, the drink consumed Dan and he and Mum split up. When he moved out of the house with the muddy bathroom floor, I moved into the small bedroom in the attic, although, as it didn't have a bed, I actually slept with Mum in her room. Then, after a while, Mum rented out the third bedroom to a series of lodgers, who seemed to come and go without incident, providing Mum with a small income for the minimum amount of hassle.

It was the first time it had been just Mum and me, but she was often too busy doing whatever it was she did to have time to bother with me. And as I hated being on my own, I was more or less forced into trying to make friends with some of the local kids. The problem was, even though I had started school by that time, I had absolutely no idea how to go about it. The way I had been brought up until then was almost feral: as long as I didn't cause Mum any trouble, I was pretty much left to do whatever I wanted. Now, all I really wanted was to have a friend. But it's hard to make friends when you don't have a clue how to socialise.

One of the things I found most difficult about any kind of interaction with other people was the fact that what they *said* often seemed to be completely contradicted by what they *did*. Because I couldn't interpret people's body language and took everything at face value, sarcasm was entirely lost on me. And because I didn't understand people's reactions, I didn't ever learn from them. So if kids were mean to me, I would be puzzled and hurt and then go back the next day and make the same mistakes all over again.

I did make one friend, after a few false starts. He was a boy who lived down the road from us, and although he teased and bullied me whenever he saw me, I kept going back and just following him around. Then, one day, he pushed me into some stinging nettles and I ran home, sobbing, with every exposed inch of my body covered in painful red rashes. I went back the next day though, and this time he let me tag along. Maybe he thought I had guts and he decided to give me a chance. But it wasn't courage that sent me back there. The way he treated me was the way I had been treated by my stepbrothers, and therefore I didn't expect anything different. And for someone as desperate as I was to have a friend, someone who ignored me was better than no one at all. So being allowed to tag along was more than I could possibly have hoped for.

I Know What You Are

For a while, I was more than happy to be someone's tag-along. It was certainly preferable to what was happening at school.

Chapter 2

On one day that I still remember quite clearly, Mum came into the school to complain because I had been physically restrained and had gone home with my arms covered in bruises. When I got really upset about something and the teachers tried to control me using physical force, I would fight back and sometimes even scratch them. I wasn't being intentionally 'bad'. Refusing to sit down or walking out of the classroom was an instinctive reaction to the sense of confusion I quickly learned would lead to a really frightening, overwhelming feeling of panic. I couldn't have described it like that at the time. All I knew was that if someone tried to force me to do something they had explained to me but that I hadn't understood, it would feel as though there was a ball of tangled, knotted wires moving around inside my head.

I Know What You Are

I thought I was just 'difficult', as Mum always said I was. And I continued to believe that, even after I was diagnosed with autism during my first year at primary school. I actually have something called Asperger syndrome, which explains why I struggled to interact and communicate with other people, and why I was unable to crack the code that would have allowed me to socialise.

People with Asperger syndrome find it difficult – or impossible – to tell other people how they feel and to interpret signs and signals like facial expressions, body language and tone of voice, which reflect someone else's mood and indicate whether they are happy, sad or angry. As a result, we don't respond appropriately and, for me, realising I've got things wrong or that I can't make sense of them at all makes me confused and hyper-anxious. So while the other kids were listening to the teachers and learning to do as they were told, I felt as though I was surrounded by people speaking a foreign language and doing random, inexplicable things.

It was a shame no one took the time to explain at least some of that to me when I was six. Maybe they did and I've just forgotten, although, even at that young age, I tended not to forget important things if they were explained to me in clear, unidiomatic terms

I could understand. Especially things that would have made me feel less guilty about all the trouble I was causing.

Going to school turned out to be the first really distressing experience of my life. To make matters worse, Mum used to threaten me with tales of a place with bars on the doors and windows where children were sent if they were taken away from their parents. 'Only good children are allowed to stay with their mums,' she used to tell me. 'Bad children have to go to the care home.'

It wasn't until quite recently that I realised what she was describing might have been a borstal, and maybe that's where she actually spent time as a young teenager, after she was kicked out by my grandma. What Mum probably didn't realise when I was six was that although I was afraid for my own sake of being sent to 'the care home', I was even more afraid for her, because I didn't know how she would cope if I wasn't there.

During my first couple of years at school, Mum was often called into meetings to discuss my behaviour. We always had terrible fights before those meetings. But as soon as we were in the presence of teachers or social workers, we would sit very close together and Mum would do all the talking, including answering most of the questions that were addressed specifically to me. In some ways, it might have been better if she had primed me beforehand by telling me exactly what to say and then letting me say it, because whenever I was forced to answer a question myself, I was terrified of saying the wrong thing. But although I have got Asperger syndrome and therefore find many aspects of social interaction very difficult to deal with, I am quite quick in other ways. So I soon learned to smile and babble away about the sort of things that might be of interest to an almost normal, reasonably happy, slightly nerdy child with an autism spectrum disorder.

Mum never actually told them about the fights that preceded those meetings. I think she preferred to communicate the information passively, by not attempting to hide the fresh scratch marks on her arms. I expect they admired her for standing by me and sympathised with her for having to try to cope with my wild behaviour. What they must have seen was a woman on her own struggling to control a physically violent six-year-old. What they *didn't* see were the painful red patches on my scalp or the clumps of my hair that had come away in Mum's hands when she pulled it so hard it brought tears to my eyes.

It seems that Mum was right about social workers though: as long as I was clean, fed and apparently not afraid to sit close to my mother during those meetings, they believed that everything must be all right. Which must have been a relief for them, because no one seemed to know what to do with us. I don't think they were used to having to deal with kids like me, although Asperger's tends to be at the less severe end of the autism spectrum, and I can't have been the only autistic child in the entire county.

The main problem I had was that, because I couldn't tell anyone what I felt or needed, I would fly off the handle whenever I was confused and frightened, which was quite a lot of the time when I was at school. Every time it happened, someone would phone Mum and ask her to come and pick me up, and I would be suspended for a couple of days.

Paradoxically, in view of the fact that the reason I was in trouble at school was always for displaying the kind of 'difficult' behaviour Mum often told me was ruining *her* life, she always took my side against the teachers. Instead of being angry with me on those occasions, she would smile at me as we walked out of the school, as though we were co-conspirators in some mischievous plot. Then we would run across the road to the park, where she would buy me an ice cream.

What probably made my continued 'bad' behaviour even more perplexing and frustrating for my teachers was the fact that the tablets that had been prescribed for me by the doctor when I was first diagnosed with Asperger's didn't seem to be doing any good. Maybe they *would* have helped calm me down a bit and made it all more manageable – for my teachers and for me – if I had been allowed to take them. But although Mum smoked weed, she didn't believe in tablets, and as soon as we got home from the doctor's surgery, she threw them all away. So I didn't ever get the chance to find out what effect they might have had.

One of my greatest fears at that time was that if I didn't learn to cope, I might actually be sent to a special school or, even worse, to one of the care homes Mum used to tell me about. And if that happened, I would be somewhere that sounded worse than school and Mum would be on her own. That was another reason for wanting to show my teachers I was clever, because then they might believe that everything was all right at home. The problem was I couldn't read. While I was struggling to try to grasp even the basic concept of reading, some of the other kids in my class were moving on from the few words they had already learned at nursery school. In the end, I was so frustrated by not being able to understand the method the teachers used and so determined to catch up with the others that I taught myself.

I accepted Mum's insistence that I was perfectly capable of being 'normal' if I just tried harder, as any six-year-old would do. But I hated it when she called me 'a retard', in a nasty, mocking voice, and when she found ways to make it clear to me that needing extra help at school was something to be ashamed of. Again, I think she hoped that if I *was* ashamed of my disabilities, I would at least learn to hide them and to present a 'normal' front to the world. So she tried – with some success – to make me afraid to be different and to learn to recognise what was 'normal behaviour', so that I could copy it.

What she didn't realise was that I *did* know, from an early age, that I wasn't the same as everyone else. I might not have been able to work out for myself what people meant by the things they said and did, but I knew, very often, that what I said and did wasn't right. The trouble was, the more I tried to be normal, the more stressed I became; and the more stressed I became, the more difficult it was for me to act normally.

Sometimes, when Mum and I were having an argument and I lost my temper, she would smirk, as though she had won, and then walk away. When I was older, I learned to dig my nails into the back of my hand and repeat silently in my head, 'I have got to keep control of this'. But for me it wasn't winning or losing a fight that really mattered; what I needed was to be able to talk about whatever had happened. Instead, I bottled everything up inside me until all the suppressed frustrations and anger reached a critical point and exploded again. It was how I felt at school too.

My constant struggle to be normal wasn't helped by the fact that, for some of the most impressionable early years of my life, I had lived with adults who treated me as an equal and were quite happy for me to argue with them. So whereas a 'normal' child confronted by an angry teacher might cry, apologise and move on, I thought the rhetorical questions I was being asked required answers. By 'talking back', I quickly gained a reputation for having a serious attitude problem, which, while possibly true, was never intentional.

After a while, whenever I was 'naughty', my teachers started sending me to the teacher who taught the 11-year-olds. He was a big man, tall and heavily built, who would tower above me with his hands behind his back and then bend down so that his face was just a few inches from mine and I could feel the damp heat of his breath as he shouted at me. He was the only teacher who could get through to me – and the only one who could make me cry. I suppose it was because his anger was so obvious and unambiguous that even an autistic six-year-old could recognise and understand it.

I hated getting into trouble at school, but the fact that it somehow brought Mum and me closer together seemed like a good thing. She had been almost a stranger to me before Dan walked out. Now though, with my stepsiblings gone too, she was the only person I had left and the only person who had any reason to be on my side. Dan still dropped by to see us from time to time, until he had an accident and died when I was eight. His death was upsetting, but not devastating, as it already felt as though Mum and I were on our own. I think Mum must have felt like that too, and that was why she started to become very possessive and controlling.

I hadn't liked it when our lives had been a chaotic shambles and Mum barely seemed to notice I was there. I didn't like it any better when it was just us and I became the sole focus of her attention. Although she wanted me to be normal, she seemed to hate me being at school, because the times she was nicest to me were when I got sent home. I know she was taken into care herself as a child. So maybe she had always felt as though she had been abandoned, and now I was the only person she might be able to hold on to. If that was true, it would also explain why she was so critical of anyone I did manage to make friends with, like the little girl who lived down the road and asked me to tea when I was seven.

It isn't until children start going to school and to friends' houses that they become aware that there are other ways of being a family and other types of behaviour that might be encouraged or disapproved of. For me, that process of being exposed to alternatives began when I went to Kelly's house.

One day, when I was playing with Kelly in her garden, her rabbit bit my finger. Kelly was really nice about it and put her arm around my shoulders as she led me into the house. Then her mum took me upstairs to the bathroom, where she put Germolene on the cut before covering it with a plaster. I remember being intrigued by what she was doing and by the kindly way she spoke to me, as if it hadn't even crossed her mind that what had happened might have been my fault. I wasn't used to being spoken to like that, or to having my wounds dressed with ointments and plasters. If I ever cut myself when we lived with Dan, he would take a Rizla out of the pack, spit on it and lay it over the cut to stop the bleeding. Then, if it became infected – by the bacteria already inside it or by those introduced in Dan's spit – he would squeeze the edges of the cut together, scrape off the pus with a credit card and then douse it with TCP. It may not have been as hygienic a process as the one used by Kelly's mum, but it was usually quite effective.

Another thing that fascinated about Kelly's family was the fact that they were vegetarians, and her mum cooked proper meals. As a child who lived primarily on takeaways, I was intrigued and impressed by the vegetables I was given for my tea. I couldn't wait to tell Mum about what I had eaten. But she just laughed at me and then took the mickey out of me about it for days afterwards. I didn't understand why at the time, although I realise now that praising someone else for doing something Mum didn't do probably felt to Mum as though I was criticising her. What I did understand, though, was that it would be better in future not to tell Mum about anything that happened at my friend's house.

However, even Kelly's mum would have found it hard to compete when it came to cleaning the house.

Mum may not have done any cooking, but once we had got away from the chaos of the doss-house and then the mess created by five children in a house that had already been listed for demolition, she became almost obsessively house proud. It was as if she had developed some sort of house-cleaning paranoia. Sometimes, she would spend hours scrubbing and polishing until every germ had been massacred and every shabby, lacklustre surface gleamed, then, a few minutes after she had finished, she would announce that we wouldn't be able to go out as we had planned because the house still wasn't clean enough and it all had to be done again. I don't know how she continued to be able to live with the bare soil in the bathroom. But, somehow, she seemed to be able to shut her mind to it and to focus instead on mopping and bleaching the concrete floor around it, which was always spotlessly clean – between rainfalls.

As well as tying Mum to the house, the cleaning created other problems for me, because whenever I made a mess, she reacted as if the end of the world had come. As I was not very well coordinated as a child, I lived in a constant state of anxiety, knowing that if I knocked over a cup of juice, Mum would be both angry and hurt. It was as if she thought I had done it deliberately, with the sole purpose of making her life more difficult than it already was. In reality, however, clumsiness was something I was prone to because of the Asperger syndrome, and added to the stress of knowing how upset Mum would be if I spilled or broke something, I was always an accident waiting to happen. So, for most of the time when I was at home, I was either banished to my room because I had already made a mess, or I had been sent to play outside so that I didn't disturb the pristine perfection Mum was always striving to achieve.

Even though it was often stressful living in the warzone Mum created in her constant battle against dirt and mess, I did benefit from the results of her hard work. I can remember going to other people's houses as a child and seeing dirty work surfaces or overflowing rubbish bins in the kitchen and thinking how lucky I was to live in our house and to have clean clothes to wear. I always had a lot of toys too, which Mum bought for me at the car-boot sales she loved going to. I was lucky in many other ways as well, particularly compared with some of the kids who lived near us. What tended to outweigh the positives, however, was the constant state of anxiety I lived in because of Mum's unpredictable, volatile moods and the fact that something she might not bat an eyelid at one day could send her into a rage the next. She didn't ever set any boundaries, even when I was very young, and for someone like me, who has real problems trying to cope with change, her inconsistency meant I was always on edge and couldn't ever relax.

It wasn't all bad though. We did have some really nice days out together, and even some holidays. One year, we had a holiday at the seaside, although, unfortunately, it didn't turn out as well as I think either of us had hoped. I tend to get fixated on things that interest me, and at that time, around the age of eight, it was old houses. Mum had promised to take me to see one that was near where we were staying and only open to the public on certain days of the year. I had read about it in a book at our local library and, for me, visiting it was to be the highlight of the whole holiday. So when the day finally came, I was so excited I could hardly contain myself.

We went by coach from the place we were staying, and almost as soon as we had sat down, Mum started chatting to the coach driver and completely ignored me. It was as if I had suddenly evaporated or become invisible. By the time we arrived at the house, the plan for our day had changed and instead of taking me to look round it, as she had promised she would do, Mum had decided to go to a pub and have a drink with the coach driver – a man she had just met and would probably never see again.

One of the problems for many people with Asperger syndrome is that they can't express their emotions. I have quite good language skills – which, again, is quite a common attribute of the condition – but I find it really difficult to identify or explain what I feel, although it's a bit easier now than it was when I was a child. So I started kicking off, and then I felt embarrassed because people were looking at me. But I couldn't stop myself. The disappointment and frustration were like a big ball of blackness expanding inside me. And I was angry too, because Mum knew how much I had been looking forward to that day, and because she had promised.

Although I wasn't tall for my age when I was a child, I was quite chubby, thanks to a diet that consisted almost exclusively of junk food, and Mum is petite and skinny. So when I lashed out at her, I probably hurt her. I know I scratched her arms. But she fought back, pushing and hitting me and shouting that I had wrecked her holiday. She said the same thing again many times afterwards, and told me how long it had taken her to save up the money to pay for it, how she had only gone on the holiday for my sake, because she knew it was something I had always wanted to do, and how I had ruined it all, just like I always ruin everything. I felt really bad about it for a long time, particularly because, even at the age of eight, I was aware that Mum couldn't really afford for us to have a holiday at all. So, in the end, it became just one more item to add to the ever-increasing list of things I felt guilty about when I was a child.

Mum and I weren't the only ones who felt sorry for Mum. Everyone else in the family did too, because of the way I behaved. It wasn't until years later that I began to understand why I often reacted the way I did, and that it didn't help me to control myself when Mum fought back, pushing and scratching me and pulling my hair. She always said it was self-defence, which was an explanation I accepted, until I became aware that most parents don't allow situations to escalate to the point of getting involved in physical fights with their children. What I really needed when my frustration exploded into panic was someone to calm me down by making me believe that, although I didn't have any control over things, they *did*, and they were going to take care of everything so that there was nothing for me to worry about. Instead, when I had a tantrum, Mum had one too.

She used to call those occasions when I got upset and lashed out 'auti moments' – short for autistic, I suppose. They happened when I felt more than usually confused or insecure, which was most of the time whenever we travelled anywhere, because Mum couldn't get off a bus or a train without instantly getting lost. She was always completely hopeless about finding the way. All children need to believe that their parents are in total control in any situation; for a child with autism, the realisation that that isn't the case is a trigger for total panic.

I remember one particular occasion, when I was about seven, when we had spent the day at the beach and were walking along the sand trying to find the bus that would take us home. Mum had no idea which bus we needed to catch, let alone which bus stop it would stop at. But she just laughed about our predicament and made no attempt to hide it from me, even though she knew how distressing I found even the thought of being lost.

Perhaps she would have had a better sense of direction and made better travel plans if she hadn't always smoked weed when we were on holiday. She said she needed it to cope with me, because I was so difficult. 'If I didn't have weed,' she told me, 'I wouldn't be able to take you on holiday at all.' Maybe that was true – although it might have been better not to have added to my anxiety by telling me so. It was certainly true that I kicked off more often than usual when we were away from home. But only because I was unnerved by being somewhere I didn't know, where everything was new and unfamiliar.

For me, almost any outing with Mum was like a nightmare, and a vicious circle: she got us lost because she was stoned; I almost imploded with distress because she didn't know where we were; she smoked more weed because I was kicking off … She thought everything was funny when she was stoned. Whereas, in those situations, I could never find anything to laugh about at all.

In the end, I took on the responsibility of knowing everything that needed to be known to enable us to do the things other parents and children take for granted – like getting home at the end of a day out. So there was a positive outcome from that day at the beach, and from all the other days when Mum couldn't find the right bus, because I learned to plan our routes in advance and to work things out for myself.

Taking on the role of route planner at the age of eight was good for me in some ways, I suppose. But there are many decisions a child isn't mentally mature enough to make. That's why children are supposed to live with responsible adults until they become adults themselves. Because if there's no one watching out for them, preventing them from making mistakes because they can't yet see the bigger picture, they can become involved in things that may destroy their childhood and affect them adversely for the rest of their lives.

Chapter 3

It was not understanding something that made me anxious. Sometimes, though, I didn't *know* that I didn't understand, so situations that might have been distressing for another child were simply a bit confusing for me, because I was used to people doing apparently inexplicable things.

An example of what I mean occurred at school when I was seven. At the end of a corridor in the school building there was a metal grille door with some stairs behind it that led up to a music studio. Some of the kids in my class had tried to open the grille, but it was too stiff and heavy for little hands. Then, one day, I was in the corridor when a boy called Billy managed to slide it back just far enough for him to squeeze through. Billy was in the top class, so he must have been 10 or 11, and when he looked straight at me and said 'Come on' I just stood there for a moment, staring at him, unable to believe he had really chosen me.

There was one large room at the top of the stairs and a door that opened into a much smaller room with a row of washbasins along one wall. There must have been toilets too, but perhaps all the doors were closed, because I don't remember them now. Billy and I were standing beside the basins when he told me to do something I didn't understand. I was so proud of being in that forbidden place with someone who had actually asked me to go with them that I felt a rush of panic at the thought that I might be about to ruin everything by getting it wrong. No one had ever chosen me for anything before, and if I messed this up, maybe no one ever would again.

Fortunately, Billy didn't seem to be as impatient as a lot of the other kids were, and after he had explained it to me again, he put his hand into the pocket of his trousers, pulled out a necklace and said, 'And then I'll give you this.'

All I remember after that is walking back down the stairs holding the necklace tightly in my hand. So I suppose I must have given him the blowjob that I only understood much later was what he described to me that day.

I showed the necklace to my mum that evening and told her, proudly, that a boy in the top class had given it to me. As she was examining it, with a half-smile, I suddenly remembered the huge row that had followed the incident with one of my stepbrothers when we lived with Dan. I still didn't know why Dan had been so angry, but some instinct told me that what had happened with Billy might be wrong in the same sort of way and that, if it was, it would be better not to tell Mum what I had done to deserve such a wonderful gift.

Mum must have thought Billy had given me the necklace simply because he liked me. So it was unkind of her to remark, as she dropped it back into my hands, that it would have cost him £1, at most. She was probably right though, because it broke a couple of days later when I was threading it through my fingers and admiring it for the hundredth time. I can still remember how disappointed I was and how fool-ish I felt for having been so proud of something that Mum had been able to identify immediately as just cheap tat.

I wasn't ever abused or badly treated in any way by any of Mum's friends when we lived in Cora's flat. But I did see things that children shouldn't see. For example, I have a very clear memory of sitting on the floor in the living room with my legs crossed and my hands in my lap, watching a couple bouncing around on top of each other on the sofa. I must have been three years old, and it was just another of the many mystifying incidents I didn't even try to understand.

For the people who were Mum's friends at that time, there weren't any boundaries between things that were sexual and non-sexual, which meant that, when I went to school, I had to learn, incident by incident, what was okay and what wasn't. So I wasn't expecting my teacher's furious reaction when she found me sitting in the classroom one day with my hand inside the trousers of the little boy next to me. What might have passed as innocent exploration at the age of three or four was viewed as something entirely more sinister at seven. In reality though, I was still very naive.

Gavin was the youngest in a family of several neglected children, most of whom were aggressive and quarrelsome. But Gavin was different, and because he was always nice to me and always stood up for me when someone teased or bullied me, he became my 'boyfriend'. After that day, however, the teacher made us sit on opposite sides of the classroom. And I learned that, for some reason, putting your hand inside someone else's trousers was not 'acceptable behaviour'.

Most of my other memories I have of school are associated with feeling confused, overwhelmed and quite lonely. There was an avenue of trees in the school grounds where I often sat on my own, picking up small stones and putting them in my pocket. Mum used to say she could tell from how many I had collected what sort of day I had had. Just a couple of stones was a sign that I had played with Gavin and some of the other kids. A whole pocketful meant I had been alone during all the playground breaks.

I sometimes felt as though I was the only person in the world. I did have a few friends by the time I was seven, but Mum didn't ever make friends with their parents. In fact, she didn't have any relationships with women while I was growing up; just with guys. So there didn't seem to be any connection between my life and the lives of anyone I knew, which meant that, in a way I can't explain, I didn't feel as though I was *part* of anything.

I can remember feeling as though there was a huge, sad sigh building up inside me – although I couldn't have explained it that way at the time – and if I started to let it out, I wouldn't ever stop sighing. The reason it was there was because I rarely understood why the teachers shouted at me and why the other kids laughed. I can't pick out any individual voices – except for the voice of the male teacher who used to shout at me – but there always seemed to be at least one angry face glaring at me, or someone sniggering and sneering at something stupid I had said or done. That was why I was always hiding – behind the bookshelves in the library, in the wings on the stage, or in the avenue of trees, picking up stones where all the other kids playing in the playground couldn't see me.

I know now, after studying child development at college, that there are two types of socialisation: primary, which children are taught at home by their parents and other members of their family, and secondary, which is what they learn at school. Apparently, if a child hasn't learned the first type, you can't expect them to understand the second. I had a huge handicap already, due to the Asperger's, and it wasn't helped by the fact that no one had ever attempted to teach me to share or take turns with other people.

When we lived in Cora's flat, Mum and her friends talked, of course, but there were no conversations, and no one ever said please or thank you. If I wanted something, I simply tugged repeatedly on someone's shirt or head-butted them until they gave it to me. But although they didn't teach me anything that would have been useful to know before I was thrown into a classroom with a lot of other kids, they didn't shout at me either, like everyone at school seemed to do.

It was the shouting that really frightened me. And when I was frightened, I panicked. As a result, I spent quite a lot of my time sitting on a wooden chair in the corridor outside the head teacher's office. Sometimes, I was in trouble because I had kicked off; more often, as I got a bit older, it was because I had walked out of the classroom with the intention of going home. I was always stopped by a teacher on those occasions, but I did escape several times when I waited until playtime and asked one of the older boys to give me a leg-up over the playground wall. When I got home, Mum would make me a sandwich and take me with her to the pub.

I was always running away, from home as well as from school. On one occasion, when I was seven and Gavin's family had moved to a house outside town, I cycled all the way there on my bike and told his parents that Mum had dropped me off at the corner of the street. Gavin's grandad was a friend of Mum's and he had driven me to Gavin's new house a couple of times and then taken me home again afterwards, which is how I knew the way. Having an almost photographic memory is one of the more useful aspects of the Asperger syndrome, and I had memorised the route without even realising I was doing it. What I wasn't so good at was understanding cause and effect or imagining how other people might react in particular situations, so I was more surprised than I should have been when Mum tracked me down and shouted at me.

Although Mum was angry with me for cycling to Gavin's house, she didn't seem to mind when I ran away from school. What she *did* object to were all the phone calls asking her to go in to discuss what could be done about my unauthorised absences. Apparently, that was why she didn't ever have a job: 'It was your fault,' she told me later. 'How could I get a job when you didn't ever stay in school for more than five minutes at a time?'

When I was eight, we moved out of the house with the muddy bathroom and into a council house in the countryside. It was a nice house, with two bedrooms and a little garden with fields behind it – a palace compared with the place we had lived in before. But it was too far out of town for me to be able to travel to my old school. So I went to a new one, on a rundown council estate where the teachers were far better equipped to deal with kids with problems, like me. In fact, a lot of the kids at my new school were far worse off than I was, in one way or another. I was still 'different' though, and I still found it difficult to fit in.

Although our house was owned by the council, it was on an estate of houses that were mostly privately owned. Our new neighbours weren't friendly towards Mum and me, and although I did make some friends, they all lived on the council estate, where the school was, several streets away. When we lived in town, Mum's friends used to drop in all the time, but they didn't have cars or money for transport. So she was very lonely at the new house too. I think we both felt very isolated, just the two of us living on our own in the middle of nowhere. Things hadn't been great before, with all the problems I had had at my previous school. After we moved to the countryside, they began to get a lot worse.

It was probably the stress – of starting at a new school for me, and of the loneliness for Mum – that caused our arguments to intensify after we moved. Loneliness was almost certainly the reason why Mum's excessive house cleaning became a full-blown obsession. She was constantly scrubbing, sweeping, vacuuming and decorating, touching up barely visible scratches on skirting boards or sanding down and repainting door frames whenever I knocked off even a flake of paint. Eventually, I became so paranoid about touching anything that I hated being in the house at all.

Because I was unnerved and distressed by change of any kind and because I wanted to spend as little time as possible at home, I was even more anxious than I had always been to have a friend. That probably explains why I started to spend time with a rather unpleasant and unhappy boy called Kieran, who lived down the road. After a slow start, I was good at reading by the time I was eight. I was certainly much better than Kieran was and I used to go round to his house to read him stories. We always sat side by side in his bedroom when I was reading to him, and I would have my hand inside his trousers, touching him the way he told me to. I didn't mind doing it; it seemed a small price to pay to have a friend, even one who wasn't particularly nice to me.

Although I was miserable in the new house, I did quite like my new school. There was another primary school that was closer to our house on the private estate, but my previous school had given me such a bad report that it wouldn't take me. So I ended up at the one a bit further away, on the council estate, which actually turned out to be a good thing, because the teachers were nice and didn't shout or push the kids around and I started to do quite well academically.

I think that, for me, part of the problem at my last school had been the fact that a lot of the other kids were well behaved and academically able. A substantial proportion of them were the children of Asian parents who took education very seriously. After I had been assessed and diagnosed with Asperger syndrome, the teachers there expected me to take the tablets I had been prescribed, then do as I was told and behave myself. When that didn't happen and I continued to be one of only very few badly behaved children, no one really knew what to do with me. At my new school, however, there were lots of kids with learning difficulties and some with severe autism. So my problems seemed fairly minimal by comparison.

It may sound like an odd thing to say, but one of the good things about my new school was that the hallways were carpeted. Just that simple fact made a huge difference to me, because it made the whole environment less noisy and therefore more manageable. The teachers seemed to understand that the cacophony of chaos can have a bad effect on a child with autism. They used to let me stay in the classroom for five minutes while all the other kids went to lunch, so that, by the time I followed them into the dining room, the corridors were empty and quiet again.

As well as having my fears taken seriously, another new experience for me was feeling that my teachers liked me, perhaps because it was apparent to them that I really did want to learn. When they had worked out what teaching method suited me best, I began to flourish. Within the space of a few weeks, I had gone from being one of the most disruptive children in my class at the old school to being what almost amounted to teacher's pet at the new one. More importantly, I no longer wanted to climb over the playground wall and run home, because school had become a refuge for me and somewhere I *wanted* to be.

I have a type of Asperger syndrome that impacts on my social skills rather than on my ability to learn. In fact, I have always found that I can absorb information quite easily and that I'm good at focusing my attention on things, although that means I sometimes get a bit fixated on subjects that particularly interest me. What I do find difficult is trying to decipher meaning and innuendo. As a child, I thought people meant exactly what they said, so I didn't understand jokes or sarcasm. I am a bit better at it now, but it's still a problem for me. What it all meant when I was at school was that unless the learning process was specifically tailored to my disabilities, so that it didn't rely on social cues, I often didn't understand what the teacher was saying.

For example, I couldn't translate idioms. So when a teacher said, 'We can't go out into the playground this morning because it's raining cats and dogs', I took it literally and looked out of the window expecting to be astonished. Then, when I saw that it was simply raining, I was baffled and bemused. I often felt lost and anxious in the classroom, because so much of teaching is about interaction, which is something I simply didn't understand.

It all became much less of a problem, though, when I started at my new school, where the teachers let me learn in my own way, using books I could work through at my own pace. Some of the teaching methods were a bit unconventional. For example, one of my teachers was dyslexic and used to have to spell everything out on a little hand-held computer. But that was just what the other kids and I needed – teachers who were prepared to mould our education to our needs, rather than trying to mould *us* to fit standard techniques that wouldn't have worked for us and would have ended up making us feel even more stupid than we already believed we were.

Suddenly, having been apparently hopeless at everything, I began to do really well, in the classroom and in all my exams at the end of the first year. I only had to read the textbook a couple of hours before I took an exam and I could remember every word and every diagram on every page I had read. The only questions I couldn't answer were the ambiguously worded ones.

Ten years ago, when I was at that school, disability legislation wasn't the big news it is today. Kids like me, who had 'problems', were side-lined and simply contained and controlled as much as possible until they were old enough to leave full-time education. So I am still very grateful to those teachers for making me realise I wasn't stupid after all.

My best subject at school was English, particularly writing stories and poems. Not even the best of my teachers could have done anything about the fact that I am hopeless with numbers, and not very good at science either. Even today, I simply don't *get* numbers. Although I can read and write down 2 + 2 + 3, the numbers are just shapes that don't make any sense to me. So I forget them immediately. However, if I write the same sum as 'two plus two plus three', it makes perfect sense. I can understand the words because I can visualise and remember them, which I can't do with numbers.

What's weird, according to all the special education people who eventually assessed me, is that despite not being able to make sense of numerals, I *can* read maps. Apparently, that meant I didn't fit into any of their categories, which made them really annoyed with me because I messed up their tests by not doing what I was expected to do. Maybe they've found out more about Asperger syndrome since then and no longer expect everyone to fit neatly into at least one of the boxes that dictate, 'If you have got *this* sort of learning disability, your brain will respond in *this* way to *this* stimulus'.

The only thing that mattered to me at the time, though, was that at least I was happy at my new school, even if I was very unhappy at home. After we moved into our new house, I started comfort eating, which was something Mum seemed to encourage. Perhaps she was trying to compensate me for the constant arguments and rows we were having. But giving me two chocolate éclairs for breakfast every day simply created new problems without solving any of my existing ones.

I was already a bit chubby, so it didn't take long for me to become obese. And because I was very ashamed of the way I looked, I started hiding at school again – not to escape being shouted at by my teachers this time, but to avoid having to do PE and expose my overweight body to the ridicule of the other, much thinner, kids. In fact, many of the kids at my school were probably underfed and quite malnourished, although of course I didn't realise that at the time.

I think it was because I was overweight that I started my periods early, when I was ten. Mum didn't ever explain what was happening, except to say 'All women do it', and I can remember feeling dirty and very embarrassed every time I bled. What made things even worse was that Mum would give me sanitary pads to take to school, which, for some reason, I had to hand over to my teacher, who put them in a cupboard in the classroom. But because I would have died rather than ask the teacher in front of the whole class if I could take one out before going to the toilet, I wore the same one all day. Inevitably, I started getting infections, which aggravated the terrible period pains I already suffered from and made me feel even more ashamed about the disgusting, inexplicable thing that was happening to my body.

Eventually, the stress of it all got so bad I stopped going to school whenever I had my period. Then my schoolwork began to suffer and I gradually lost the prized, confidence-boosting academic position I had held near the top of the class.

I was still coping though, most of the time. And then, in my last term, when I had just turned 11, my class paid a visit to the secondary school I would be moving on to after the summer holidays. My first impression was that there didn't seem to be any proper school building, just a collection of pre-fabs with large windows and echoing hallways. But it was what was happening inside the buildings that made me anxious. There were about 60 kids in every class-room making a noise that seemed to reverberate off every solid surface. I knew within minutes of arriving at that school that I wasn't going to be able to manage there.

It was a sign of how comfortable I was with the teachers at my primary school that I talked to one of them after that visit and told her how I felt. As a result, it was decided that someone would try to find out whether there were any alternative arrangements that could be made for me. What I think it needed, too, was for Mum to push on my behalf. But she didn't do things like that. I don't know if anyone did try to make other arrangements for me. If they did, it never came to anything. And it didn't really matter, as things turned out, because by the time the new term started, my childhood had been halted dead in its tracks and everything had changed.

Once the last term ended, I didn't see any of the kids from my primary school anymore. The area I lived in was very strongly class divided: the private-estate and council-estate kids didn't go to the same schools and didn't mix outside school either. So I didn't know any of the kids who lived near me, and none of my friends from school ever came to the private estate where I lived. I suppose it was mutual segregation – the class barrier worked both ways.

During term time, I used to go down to the council estate on my bike to see friends. But it wasn't an area most people would have chosen to walk through, because there was a lot of tension due to the gang culture that existed there. Although I was too young to attract much attention, I had begun to feel a bit uncomfortable as an outsider, even before the summer holiday started. None of us kids had mobile phones, so I couldn't simply phone a school friend and arrange to meet somewhere else. And as Mum hadn't made friends with any of the other mums, there was nothing to help keep those relationships alive. So, at the end of the school year, I suddenly lost all my friends and had nothing to do except hang around at home, getting under Mum's feet.

It was one thing not really wanting me to go to school in case she needed company during the day, which she did a lot after we moved to the new house and she lost her social network. It was quite another having me there all the time, whether she wanted company or not, and during that summer holiday she seemed forever to be telling me to go away and leave her alone. I walked for miles that summer, on my own, through the tunnel that ran under a half-finished motorway and out across the fields into open countryside. I did it just to get out of the house. Then, one day, I made a friend, and suddenly I no longer felt as though I was the only person in the world.

Evie lived with her boyfriend and two children in a flat in one of the few other council-owned houses on the private estate, just a few doors away from us. She had been badly abused as a child and had learning difficulties. So although she was 18 when I met her, she seemed younger, and certainly wasn't capable of looking after her children on her own.

Evie's little girl, Zoe, was two years old, and the baby just a few months. I wasn't very interested in the baby, although I did feel sorry for her having to lie for hours in a filthy nappy before Evie seemed to notice and bothered to do anything about it. But I did love Zoe, and often when I took her home with me. I would take her little sister too. Surprisingly, Mum would sometimes help me bath them and then look after the baby while I played with Zoe, which was a relief because the baby cried a lot. I think it was the fact that the children were dirty that triggered her mothering instincts, because, to her, keeping your children clean is a mother's primary, perhaps only, responsibility.

What I really liked doing was taking just Zoe home with me. On the days when that happened, I would ransack the house for coins and take her to the second-hand shop in town to buy her some new clothes out of the 50p bucket. Then we would go to the public toilets, where I would change her into them before taking her to the park, all dressed up and looking nice.

That was all I did for most of that summer, go on long walks on my own and babysit for Zoe. I continued to babysit for her when the new term started. I don't think anyone ever really believed I was going to go to the secondary school. I wasn't aware of anyone from social services coming to look for me, although

I suppose someone must have done. They must have contacted Mum too, but, again, I don't remember her saying anything about it. She certainly never asked me *why* I wasn't going to school. So, somehow, I just slipped under the radar. For the next few months, Mum cleaned the house and did whatever else she was doing and I spent most of my days with Evie or Zoe, out of Mum's hair and happy not to be on my own.

In fact, I developed a crush on Evie. She was child-like in many ways and I was very naive, so it wasn't until much later that I realised she was far more sexually aware than I understood at the time. We often used to play-fight. I would chase her around her flat and when I caught up with her she would pretend to grope me. Her boyfriend, Tom, never said very much, but he would often watch us mucking about. It was for his sake she was doing it, of course. But I didn't know that, any more than Evie knew that what she was doing would turn out be a big mistake, for both of us.

Chapter 4

Tom, Evie and their kids would sometimes come round to our house and Tom would offer to cook supper for us all. Mum has never been very articulate when it comes to saying what she wants. So when they turned up at the front door, uninvited, with Tom holding carrier bags full of ingredients for the meal he wanted to make, she just shrugged and let them in.

I loved having people in the house again, instead of it just being Mum and me. Usually, it was more like a shrine to cleaning products than a home, and I liked sitting at the kitchen table listening to everyone talking and laughing, even if it was only for a couple of hours. Despite her apparent indifference, I think Mum liked it too, because she was at least as lonely as I was. She probably would have preferred it if Evie and Tom had come without the kids though, and if I hadn't been there either.

'You know why he comes round here, don't you?' she would often say to me after they had gone. 'He's sniffing round you. It's obvious what he's after.' I had no clue what she meant. I was 11 years old and no one had ever explained to me about the birds and the bees. Although I had seen people having sex when I was very young, I had only recently found out where babies come from, by reading an article in one of Evie's magazines, which actually left me more bemused than informed. And anyway, although I quite liked Tom, it was Evie I was infatuated with.

Tom was obviously crazy about her too. What he didn't know, however, was that while he was at work, Evie often saw other men. Living in that town, it was a secret she wasn't going to be able to keep forever, and eventually people began to gossip. But it was Zoe who gave it away in the end. If I wasn't available to babysit, Evie had to take the children with her when she went to meet whatever guy she was currently seeing behind Tom's back. When Tom got home from work one evening and asked Zoe what she had been doing all day, she told him, and then added, 'And Mummy was kissing a man at the bus stop.'

After things began to go wrong between them, Tom started coming round to our house on his own. He would cry as he talked about their relationship and how he really wanted to work things out with Evie, and I would do my best to comfort him. Then I would tell him about the latest row I had had with Mum and he would sympathise with me and tell me that whatever had happened wasn't my fault. Gradually, as we became closer, I started to believe that he was the only person who really understood me. Until then, it had always been Mum and me against the rest of the world. Now, it was Tom who was my only real friend and ally.

Sometimes he came round to our house just after I had had a screaming argument with Mum and had retreated to my bedroom, slamming the door and turning my music up as loud as it would go. Tom would have a cup of tea with Mum and then come upstairs and sit with me on the bed, listening while I told him what had happened, then smoothing my damp hair and telling me everything was going to be okay. Mum isn't the sort of person who gives comfort or cuddles, or even brief hugs. When I was angry or upset, her reaction was to shout even more loudly than I was doing, and I always ended up feeling worse than I had done to begin with. So it was a new, and very pleasant, experience to be listened to and sympathised with.

I don't really know what sort of relationship there was between Tom and Mum, or if there was any particular reason why she would storm out of the house if he came up to my room without first stopping to have a cup of tea with her. She didn't like anyone giving me attention that could have been paid to her. So it may simply have been jealousy and there may have been nothing between them at all. Perhaps her reaction was just another facet of the many tensions that existed at that time as a result of the complicated cross-relationships between Evie, Tom, Mum and me.

I still wasn't going to school. I spent most days with Zoe, waiting for Tom to finish work so that we could go on a bike ride or hang out together. Despite the fact that there was an age difference of more than ten years between us, Tom was the best friend I had ever had. But then something happened that changed our relationship and made everything even more complex and confusing than it already was.

It was an evening in December and I was in my bedroom wrapping Mum's Christmas present when Tom knocked on the door and came in. I was already in my nightie and when he touched the bow on the front of it, his hand rested on my boob just long enough for me to notice but without it seeming weird. Then he started talking about Christmas and I probably wouldn't have remembered what he had done if it had remained an isolated incident. In fact, things escalated so slowly after that night I hardly noticed what was happening.

At first, it was just rough and tumble, the sort of games a brother and sister or any other kids might play. Then one day he kissed me, on another day he lifted up my top to look at my boobs, and before long I believed that we were 'in a relationship'. He never put pressure on me to do anything I didn't want to do. If I tried to turn away while he was kissing me, for example, he always stopped immediately. He did everything in a way that made me believe, at 11 years old, that it was what *I* wanted. And when he asked me to do things I didn't want to do, I did them because I wanted to please him and because I was tired of being lonely and he was my only friend.

I can only remember one occasion when Tom tried to force me to do something I didn't want to do. It wasn't long after he had kissed me for the first time. We were in the garden of his mum's house when he suddenly grabbed my hand and pushed it down inside his trousers. I had touched boys of my own age at primary school, but never a man before, and I was really shaken. When I tried to pull my hand away, Tom grabbed my arm and held it where it was. I was more confused than frightened, until I saw the dark, almost threatening look in his eyes. By the time he released his grip, his fingerprints had left little red marks on my skin, which slowly turned into bruises.

I didn't have any concept that what he was doing was wrong. I had read articles in Evie's magazines about little girls whose dads crept into their bedrooms at night and did horrible things to them that traumatised and scarred them for the rest of their lives. And I had read about women who were raped – usually by men they didn't know – who were very frightened and struggled to try to get away. But what Tom was doing to me wasn't anything like what had happened to the little girls and women in those magazine stories. Tom didn't ever hurt me and I wasn't afraid of him. I often felt embarrassed by what he did to me, but only because I didn't have real breasts, like Evie did, and I thought he must be comparing me to her and would soon realise I wasn't really worthy of his attention.

I read a lot as a child. It seems odd when I think about it now, but I was probably reading Harry Potter during the time when I was becoming involved in a 'relationship' with Tom. Reading was a form of escapism for me – I *loved* the Harry Potter books. But there weren't any books, or even television programmes, that involved an 11-year-old girl having a relationship with an adult man. At least, there weren't any that I saw or was aware of at that time. So I decided that what Tom was doing was something private, something lots of people do, but don't talk about. I think I knew that wasn't true, although I certainly had no idea that it was abuse. But when you've spent your life not understanding a lot of the things people do, it's sometimes easier to tell yourself a lie rather than become fixated on trying to work it out.

Eventually, when I did begin to suspect that it might be wrong in some way, I started researching rape on the computer. But I still didn't make the connection with what Tom was doing to me. In fact, it wasn't until a couple of years later that I finally understood.

When I was 13, there was a storyline on *EastEnders* based on Bianca's boyfriend's abuse of her teenage stepdaughter, Whitney. Although Whitney didn't *want* to have sex with Tony, he didn't actually rape her. He groomed her, by being nice to her and making her feel special when she did the things he wanted her to do. So when Bianca found out what was happening, Whitney was really upset, because she didn't want to lose him.

I was glued to the TV as the storyline developed, and I can remember feeling an almost physical sense of shock when I realised that what was happening between Tony and Whitney was what had happened between Tom and me. It was the first time I had ever seen or heard anything to suggest that there was a type of rape that wasn't forceful. But as I didn't have the mental capacity at 13 to think it all through, and there was no one I could have talked to about it, I eventually just put it to the back of my mind and tried to forget about it.

It's normal, apparently, in situations like Whitney's and mine, to put a positive spin on something negative or something that doesn't seem to make any sense. For example, instead of thinking 'I am being abused/raped', you turn it around and tell yourself, 'This is happening because I am special. He is doing this because he loves me and can't wait.' It was a delusion Tom reinforced every time he told me, 'I know I should wait until you're 16 and we can get a place together, but I can't help myself. It's because I care so much about you.'

Even when Mum threatened to tell someone about what was happening, I kept reassuring myself, 'It's okay because he really loves me. It wouldn't be fair to grass him up. It's my fault for leading him astray when he's trying to do the right thing and wait.' That I was to blame for it was an explanation that came easily to me because I believed almost everything was my fault; it was what Mum had been telling me for as long as I could remember. It was my fault for crying all the time when I was a baby and ruining her life. It was my fault for having temper tantrums on holidays she couldn't really afford. It was my fault for getting her hauled into school for meetings about my behaviour. It was my fault for dropping a cup of tea and messing up the house it had just taken her hours to clean … There was an almost endless list of negative things I was responsible for. Leading Tom astray was just something else to be added to it. What was more powerful than my guilt about my 'relationship' with Tom, however, was my need to have *someone* to love me and think I was special.

When Tom started coming round to our house on his own, we would sit together under a blanket on the sofa in the living room, watching television, and he would touch me intimately, while Mum became increasingly restless and irritable. Eventually, she would snap at me, 'What are you doing? You're disgusting, Taylor,' and then storm out of the room.

The fact that she didn't ever ask Tom what *he* was doing, or tell him to stop what she knew was going on, simply reinforced my belief that, basically, it was okay and she was just angry with me because she was jealous that I was getting all Tom's attention.

As the weeks went by, I became trapped in a situation I didn't really like but that I didn't see any way out of. I don't think I really wanted to get out of it, because I was prepared to do whatever would make Tom happy, for his own sake and so that I didn't lose my only friend. I was 11 years old. I didn't know that what he was doing was wrong, and even if I had suspected that it was, I had already learned that it was better not to trust my own instincts. And after all, if there really had been a problem, surely Mum would have been angry with Tom and would have told him to stop coming round.

It's difficult to explain to someone who 'gets' irony and can interpret social interactions what it's like to grow up in a state of permanent bewilderment and confusion. I was bright, in an academic way: I was interested in facts and could read and absorb quite complex information from a young age – as long as it didn't involve numerals! But I had no idea at all about what made other people tick or why one thing was right and something else was wrong. If you're lucky, those are the sort of things you learn from your parents. But, as well as having all the handicaps associated with Asperger syndrome, I didn't have anyone I could rely on for moral guidance, or for any other kind of behavioural regulation.

Perhaps Mum didn't know what was right and what was wrong any more than I did. Maybe that's why she just laughed when Tom teased me and did things like pulling my trousers down in front of her. But she must have been able to see how humiliated and embarrassed I was, even if she didn't actually know that it was inappropriate for a man in his twenties to be doing that to a little girl.

When our 'relationship' deepened and Tom became less able to control his feelings for me – as I believed – we had anal sex in my mum's bed when she was out. I didn't know what he was doing when he turned me over and lay on top of me. He was very gentle, so although it was uncomfortable, it didn't actually hurt. It was horrible afterwards though, because instead of sitting with his arm around me, as he usually did when we had been kissing and cuddling, he stood up without saying a word and went into the bathroom, almost slamming the door behind him.

I had read enough about sex by that time to have a vague idea of what was involved, and I was pretty sure he hadn't put his penis where it was supposed to go. So I thought I must have done something wrong and that he had left the bedroom without speaking to me because he was cross with me or, worse, upset. When he still didn't say anything, or even look at me, when he eventually came out of the bathroom, I was mortified because I knew I was right.

My reaction to what happened that day was to be really anxious to do it properly the next time. But, for some reason I didn't understand, I kept on getting it wrong. Every time Tom did it, he would suddenly stop, then go into the bathroom and shut the door. When he came out again, he didn't look at me and always left without saying a word, leaving me feeling stupid and worthless. He was my friend and I wanted him to be happy, but I couldn't even do that one small thing to please him. Looking back on it now, I realise that he probably felt guilty and ashamed of what he was doing – although not guilty and ashamed *enough* not to do it again the next time I was alone in the house when he came round.

Even at school, I had always wanted to do the right thing. But I never seemed to be able to work out what the right thing was. So I was used to people being annoyed with me or winding me up by saying things they knew I wouldn't understand because I didn't know the difference between the truth, a lie and a joke. 'Look!' someone might say to me, pointing to the sky. 'It's a pink aeroplane.' And while I ran to the window to search the clouds for a flash of pink, they all laughed at me for being so stupid.

I suppose it was a combination of my extreme naivety and eagerness to please, plus the fact that my mum didn't protect me, that made me an ideal victim – first for Tom and then for all the men who came after him.

I did try to talk to Mum eventually about what was happening with Tom. But I couldn't get the words out and I burst into tears before I had really told her anything. I think she must already have had some idea what was going on though, because all she said, calmly and quite firmly, was, 'It's okay. I'll make sure he stays away from you.'

The next time I saw Tom was in town. Mum and I had gone in together to do some shopping and when he came over to talk to us she just glared at him and didn't answer. But that didn't help at all, because then I felt guilty about upsetting him and anxious in case he guessed that I had said something to her. To try to cover up my confusion and embarrassment, I agreed when he suggested that, if Mum had done all the shopping she wanted to do, I might like to go with him while he did his. Mum just turned around and walked away without saying anything, but I could tell she was angry. She was still angry when I got home. 'Okay,' she told me, 'you've made your decision. I offered to help you, but you obviously don't want my help. So that's it. You're on your own now.' Then she stormed out of the room, leaving me feeling very guilty and unhappy because, apparently, I had had a choice between Mum and Tom and I seemed to have chosen Tom.

I found anything emotional completely exhausting. I felt sorry for Tom because Mum was angry with him. I felt guilty for telling Mum about what Tom was doing – or, at least, for crying and trying to tell her. And I felt guilty because Mum thought I had chosen Tom instead of her. All that guilt and emotion, when all I really wanted was for Tom to stop doing what he was doing to me and – even more than that – not to be on my own.

Tom's relationship with Evie had pretty much fallen apart by that time. I suppose it was because Mum had given up on me that she didn't seem to be bothered when he started staying round at our house most nights. She knew we were sleeping together, on the floor of the living room. In fact, she brought us cups of tea every morning, although she did plonk them down on the floor beside us without speaking. But she just let us get on with it.

It was someone else who eventually phoned the police to raise concerns about our relationship. I didn't ever find out who it was, but I suspect it was a neighbour – or possibly even Evie – rather than someone in the family. It certainly wasn't Mum. She would never willingly have got the police involved in anything, particularly in something that could lead to all sorts of hassle for her, with social services and the education authority asking questions about why I hadn't spent a single day at secondary school.

The first Mum or I knew about it was when two police officers turned up at the house one day. They asked Mum some questions about me and, I think, about Tom, and although she didn't give much away, I could see that she was rattled. Then one of the police officers turned to me and asked, 'Is there anything you want to tell me?'

There wasn't any reason for her to have known that I have Asperger syndrome, or to have understood what it meant, specifically. So, even if she had known, she would probably have asked me the same question, without realising it wouldn't elicit much information from someone like me. In my mind, a question phrased like that required a simple 'Yes' or 'No' answer. There were plenty of things I *could* have told her, and plenty that it would have been a good idea to tell her, from a child protection point of view. But I didn't actually *want* to tell her anything, for several reasons: because I didn't know her and therefore had no reason to believe I could trust her, because I didn't want to get Tom into trouble and because I thought I might be to blame for it all anyway, and it didn't seem like a good idea to tell a police officer about something that might be your fault.

If she had asked me a specific question about what was happening, I think I would have answered it, because I do tend to be truthful. Also, I was very unhappy by that time, although perhaps not for the reason one might expect. I must have been almost 12, and starting to grow up a bit, and I was tired of always having to be kept hidden, like some secret Tom was ashamed of. I wanted to be like the couples I saw on television and walking hand in hand in real life. We could be a couple at home or when we went out together on bike rides in the countryside. But everywhere else we had to walk slightly apart, sometimes completely separately, so that no one who saw us would suspect that we were together.

Although I was convinced that we were in a relationship, it sometimes made me anxious when some bit of information or something I had read seemed to contradict the reality I had created in my mind. The conflict was confusing, and it was unnerving to have to defend 'my truth' – if only to myself – and reshape it constantly as I became aware of new facts about the real world.

I believed, too, that Tom really did love me and that we were going to be together, openly and permanently as he always promised, as soon as I was 16. The visit from the police threatened those beliefs and made me anxious. Fortunately though – or so I thought at the time – when I answered the police officer's question by saying that there was nothing I *wanted* to tell her, she simply accepted what I had said and they left without asking me anything further.

Maybe it *was* Evie who made the phone call that prompted that visit from the police. It could have been sour grapes, because she was jealous that Tom was seeing someone else – even if that 'someone else' was just a child who used to be her friend. But maybe she was actually concerned for my welfare. That's what I would like to believe, although in reality, with the best will in the world, I don't think Evie had the mental or moral capacity to make a judgement like that.

Whoever it was, and whatever their intentions for doing it, the only result it had as far as I was concerned was to make me even more paranoid in my belief that everyone was trying to steal Tom away from me – Mum, maybe Evie, the police, our neighbours. Well, they weren't going to succeed. I wasn't going to allow other people to put their own narrow-minded inter-pretation on my relationship with Tom. Whatever the rights or wrongs of it, he was kinder to me than anyone had ever been before. At 11 years old, I believed I was madly in love with him and that he loved me and that, together, we could take on all the people who had their own mean-spirited reasons for not wanting us to be happy. I suppose it was another example of self-protection by putting a positive spin on something negative or baffling, because I would have been incredibly hurt if I had known the truth.

It was around the time when the police came to our house that Evie and Tom's already very damaged relationship finally fell apart completely. One day, after Tom had violently assaulted her, Evie took out an injunction against him. And as our house was just a few doors away from the flat where she was still living with the children, it meant he couldn't visit me at home anymore either.

Mum blamed me for their break-up. She said I was always coming on to him – at 11 years old! She was angry with me, she said, because it wasn't fair of me to have split them up when there were two young children involved. I thought she was right – that he had left Evie and his children because of me and that it was just one more bad thing I was guilty of.

Tom had moved into a flat in town when he and Evie initially split up, and now that he couldn't come to our house, I started visiting him there. It was a shared flat, so we didn't really *do* anything, because by the time he got back from work, there was always someone else around. I would go there in the evenings and after I had run him a bath and then washed his back while he told all about his day, we would sit together in his bed watching TV, like the couple I imagined we were. Although I liked spending time with Tom, I didn't really like going to that flat. As well as being a bit dirty, it was creepy and sleazy, in a way I couldn't really have explained.

When I was there one evening, Tom showed me some porn magazines. I thought the pictures were horrible, and confusing too, because none of the people in them seemed to be doing what Tom had done to me on several occasions in Mum's bed when she was out. One of the magazines was full of pictures of curvy girls. Although I was plump at that time, I didn't have any curves, and I suddenly realised that all the photographs were of adult women. So maybe what Tom and I had been doing wasn't all right after all, because however grown-up I might sometimes think I was, I wasn't a woman; I was just a fat child.

Those magazines only added to the doubts I already had about myself and my relationship with Tom. I began to feel a huge pressure to grow up quickly, because that was the only way I thought I might be able to get out of the situation I was in. But the idea of anything changing scared me too. I didn't have a social worker or a teacher or any friends to discuss things with. I did have Mum, but she always seemed to be angry with me, for some reasons that I understood and some that I didn't. The one thing I did feel sure about – rightly or wrongly – was that Mum didn't really want me. So Tom had been my whole life for the past year. He was the only person I could talk to, and if I didn't have him, I wouldn't have anyone at all. That was the reason why I couldn't admit – even to myself – that our relationship was wrong, because then I would be left with noth-ing, and being on my own was always one of my greatest fears.

A couple of months later, the decision was taken out of my hands – not that it had ever really been my decision to make – because Tom met someone else and moved away. He didn't tell me he was leaving. His flat was quite some distance from where we lived. So he would send a text to my mum when he wanted to see me and I would cycle into town to meet him so that we would ride back to his place together. Then, one day, the messages stopped coming.

I kept asking Mum if she had heard from him, and eventually she got really angry with me. 'Their marriage broke down because of you,' she shouted at me. 'You've destroyed their kids' lives. It's because of you that those poor kids haven't got their father around anymore.' She was really angry with me, and I felt terrible about it – because I believed that it *was* my fault, and because she seemed to hate me for what she thought I had done.

Thinking about it now, I do wonder if she had been having a relationship with Tom too. It would explain why she was so furious with me – if she thought *she* had lost him because of me. Or maybe she blamed me in some convoluted way for the fact that my dad had left her, if that's what happened when he found out she was pregnant. Or maybe my dad went off with someone else. Or perhaps her dad did. The possibilities are endless, and I'll never know the real reason, because Mum doesn't 'do' discussions.

Tom did come back a few times, but to see Mum, not me. He barely spoke to me at all, and I can remember wondering what I had done wrong. I felt quite resentful about it too, because one of the main reasons I had continued to stay away from school was so that I would be there every day when he came home from work, ready to make him a cup of tea and then cuddle up with him on the sofa to watch a movie. He had been incredibly upset when he found out Evie was seeing other men. So he must have known how I would feel now that he didn't want *me* anymore. But he simply ditched me, without any explanation or excuse. In my mind, at least, we *had* been in a relationship, and his callous dumping of me gave rise to a lot of adult emotions I wasn't really equipped to process and deal with.

I found everything difficult to cope with after I lost touch with Tom, and I was very lonely. Mum was usually out all day, and I spent a lot of time on my own at home, listening to break-up songs with tears streaming down my face, or playing half-heartedly on my PlayStation, not caring if I won or lost. The one saving grace in my life at that time was Zoe. Evie and the two children still lived in the flat they had all lived in with Tom, just a few doors away from our house. And although she and I weren't friends anymore, she was still happy to hand Zoe over to me whenever she had better things to do than look after her, which seemed to be quite a lot of the time. I was happy to have the little girl's company. I used to put her in her buggy, walk the three miles into town and then wander around the park with her, trying not to think about the fact that I had been the cause of her losing her father, because I hadn't been good enough for Tom. It was comforting to be where there were other people though. And it was while I was at the park with Zoe one day that I met Rajan.

Chapter 5

Rajan was Kurdish. He had only been in England for about six months and although he didn't speak much English, we managed to communicate quite well. I still felt as though I was going through the break-up of my relationship with Tom, and when Rajan tried to kiss me in the park one day, I felt really uncomfortable. I was shocked too, not because I realised that there was anything wrong with a 27-year-old man trying to kiss a 12-year-old girl, but because it didn't seem right for him to be doing it in front of little Zoe. Despite having only a very hazy idea of what was okay and what wasn't in terms of my relationships with other people, I was adamant that I didn't want to play around while she was with me. In fact, although it was nice to have someone to talk to, I went to the park to play with

Zoe and that was all I really wanted to do while I was there.

After that first attempt to kiss me, Rajan kept asking me to go to the park on my own, and when I eventually agreed and went there alone one afternoon, he kissed me and touched me. I didn't like what he was doing. It made me feel embarrassed and uneasy. Although I didn't really know anything about Rajan, and I didn't usually pick up on things that lay below the surface with people, I had a sense that he was like a tightly wound coil and might explode into anger if I said the wrong thing. I don't suppose I would have noticed it at all if it hadn't been for the fact that he was a bit like my mum in that respect. He had the same sort of tension inside him and his eyes didn't always smile when his mouth did. But my experiences at primary school had taught me to be wary of upsetting people in case they shouted at me and I was quite scared of him, which is why I didn't have the courage to tell him to stop.

In fact, I didn't really like Rajan. I certainly didn't feel the same way about him as I had done about Tom. I know it sounds odd to say this, considering the circumstances of my relationship with Tom, but I always felt safe when I was with him. Whereas

Rajan had a slightly predatory, boy-approaching-girl attitude towards me that I didn't like at all.

I looked as young as I was, or even younger, but when I told him, the first time we met, that I was 12 years old he said that was a good thing, because it meant that I was a virgin. I didn't really know why that would matter to him, until I eventually gave in to his constant pressure and thinly-veiled bullying and went back to his flat one day. I had only ever had anal sex with Tom, so it really was the first time for me. But, for some reason, I didn't bleed.

Rajan was angry with me afterwards, shouting at me and calling me dirty. Suddenly, he didn't look handsome at all, with his lips pulled into a thin line of disgust, and he yelled at me, 'You are not a virgin! Why do you lie to me? How many men did you sleep with?'

I was frightened by his reaction and by his obvious revulsion. He was the second man I had been inti-mate with and the second man who had been angry with me afterwards. Once again, I thought I had done something wrong and felt as ashamed as if I really had had sex with countless other men, as Rajan seemed to be so convinced I had.

Unfortunately, I was very unworldly – even for a 12-year-old – and easily intimidated, so I didn't have the confidence to walk away. Instead, I went back to his flat the next time he asked me – which he did a couple of days later, despite his apparent disgust – and on many occasions after that. I didn't agree to go because having sex with Rajan was a pleasant experience. It never was. In fact, I didn't ever *feel* anything, except for a strange sensation that I can only describe as like watching from outside my own body. Perhaps it was an early sign of the dissociation I began to experience much later as a reaction to extreme stress.

It's an odd feeling being with someone who wants to have sex with you but doesn't seem to like you. Obviously, I've only experienced life from my own perspective as someone with Asperger's, so I don't know how someone else would feel in that situation, or if anyone else would keep going back the way I did. Because Rajan wasn't kind to me in any way. He always insisted that I had to have a shower at his flat before we had sex. And as the water was always cold and he wouldn't allow me to touch his towels, I had to stand, naked and shivering, afterwards until my body had dripped dry. I wasn't permitted to eat in his flat either, I assumed for the same reason – because he thought I was dirty and didn't want me soiling his plates and cutlery. Looking back on it now, I think it wasn't only me that disgusted him. I think he was disgusted by himself too. That would explain why he was always angry with me after we had had sex, and why he sometimes pushed me around aggressively and said nasty, hurtful things.

It's unnerving not being able to understand other people's reactions. There are lots of things very young children can't make any sense of. But because they don't yet have any conscious concept of cause and effect or of being *able* to work things out for themselves, they don't even try. For someone with autism, however, knowing that you need to be able to read and interpret people's reactions but not being able to do so is frustrating, and often very disheartening. So I was confused by the contradictory way Rajan treated me: on the one hand, he often said unkind things to me; on the other, I knew that he *must* care about me, otherwise he wouldn't want to have sex with me. Ultimately though, because I believed he was my boyfriend, I simply accepted it all and told myself it was stupid to allow any of it to upset me. But even if you manage not to be actively upset by something like that, you can't do anything about the fact that it creates a little empty hole in your soul.

It was because I believed Rajan and I were in a relationship that I pushed Tom away when he came round to our house one day and tried to kiss me. 'It wouldn't be right,' I told him, probably echoing something I had heard someone say on the TV. 'I'm going out with someone else now.' That's how grown-up I thought I was. I had learned what I knew about 'love and relationships' from the TV and magazines and, at the age of 12, I was worried about cheating on one abuser by kissing another.

I don't know how Rajan justified our relationship to himself. Perhaps he didn't even bother trying. I do know that his friends objected to it. Although they always spoke their own language in front of me, they gesticulated a lot when they were talking and I could tell the first time they met me that they disapproved and were arguing with him. But Rajan just shrugged his shoulders and said something that made some of them laugh.

I often caught his friends looking at me after that, usually with expressions of contempt, and they used to send him texts telling him to meet them in the park, but always on his own. I know they wanted him to stop seeing me and I resented them and felt hurt at the time. Looking back on it now though, I realise that his friends had a morality Rajan didn't share.

One day, he told me that he was going to take me to a nightclub. I was incredibly excited. Somehow, I managed to persuade Mum that I needed some new clothes, and her friend Sid offered to take me shopping in town. Sid was quite a bit older than Mum and a genuinely nice man who was always very good to me. I think I told him I had been invited to a party with some friends who were a couple of years older and that I wanted to impress them. He was obviously a bit worried about it and when he quizzed me, quite gently, I admitted that they could be as old as 15 or even 16, which didn't sound great when I was just 12, but was considerably better than the truth. I don't think Sid approved, but he still took me shopping.

I really enjoyed spending that day with him. It was just the two of us, and after he had bought me some cropped cargo pants and make-up, he took me out for lunch. We didn't ever do it again though, because when we got home Mum accused Sid of 'sniffing around' me and they had a huge row. 'Why on earth is he spending money on you? What does he *really* want from you?' she shouted at me afterwards, as if it had all been my idea for Sid to take me shopping, when in fact she was the one who had set it up so that she didn't have to be bothered with it herself. Her reaction was ironic too, when you think that she didn't ever ask me where I had been or who I had been with when I was having sex with Rajan at his flat.

Mum's anger ruined what had otherwise been a really nice day for me. And although Sid was very offended by what she was implying, it did make him think about how it might appear to other people. And I suppose it was because he was wary of being labelled a nonce that he never took me out alone again. It was a shame, for both of us – for Sid because he wasn't able to have children of his own and had obviously enjoyed playing the role of someone's dad, and for me because I didn't *have* a dad and had enjoyed being treated like a daughter.

The other bad thing about that whole incident was that Rajan didn't take me to a nightclub after all. I don't know what made me think he would. I'm sure I wouldn't have been allowed in anyway, being a 12-year-old who looked even younger, even when I was all dressed up in my new clothes and make-up. But I didn't realise that at the time, and I was very disappointed.

Mum didn't have real boyfriends, as far as I'm aware. So she and Sid were only ever friends. At least, that's what she always swore was the case, with Sid and with all the other men who drifted in and out of her life. Most of them didn't stick around for very long. Mum does a lot of banter with men and insults them in a way I think they find amusing at first, but that eventually starts to get under their skin, so they stop seeing her. But Sid was different from most of the others. He had a sarcastic sense of humour and could easily hold his own with Mum. In fact, some of the things he said could be quite harsh and he made me cry on at least a couple of occasions – once, by calling me fat. It wasn't malicious at all. He was a middle-aged man without a wife or daughters and he didn't realise how sensitive girls of my age are about things like that. I know he was devastated when I burst into tears. In fact, he was so upset that he went out and bought me some chocolates to try to make amends – which was a very kind gesture, although perhaps not the best choice of present for someone you've just called fat!

Mum had another long-term friendship, with a guy called Derek who ran a charity shop. In fact, it was Derek who provided me with most of my clothes when I was a child, except for the ones Mum bought for me on the rare occasions when she took me shopping in town. Mum spent a lot of time at Derek's shop and when I went down there with her, he would let me rummage through the bags of clothes that had just come in and pick out any odds and ends I wanted. Most of the clothes I chose were too big for me, so made me feel less self-conscious about my body.

Because I thought I had boobs – although it was actually just puppy fat – I wore push-up bras and low-cut tops, either with cargo pants or maxi skirts, to cover up my legs, which I was *really* self-conscious about.

I had only been seeing Rajan for a few weeks when social services began to take an interest in me. I think Mum got a letter asking why I wasn't attending school. There were periods during my childhood when I don't remember Mum being there at all. It's possible that she *was* there, physically if not emotionally, and I just don't remember the things that she said and did. But I do know that I rarely saw her at that particular time. I used to go out – to the park or to Rajan's flat – as soon as I woke up in the mornings and come home on the last bus at night. So I don't know if she actually had a visit from social services. All I do know is that she told me one day that a taxi would be coming to the house the following morning to pick me up and take me to school. I can't remember whether she actually threatened me with the care home on that occasion – as she still often did when I refused to do something she had told me to do. But I do remember realising that it wasn't something that was open for discussion, and that, this time, I didn't have any choice.

I *hated* that school. It was a special school for children with a whole range of learning difficulties and physical disabilities. Asperger syndrome is at the lower end of the autism spectrum, and although people with it can have specific difficulties such as dyslexia, dyspraxia or attention deficit disorder, they tend not to have the same kind of learning disabilities that accompany many other types of autism. But, despite the fact that I didn't have any problems with learning, I was put in a class for severely autistic children. I suppose no one knew what else to do with me. The schools for 'naughty' kids won't take anyone who hasn't been in the care system or in trouble with the police. And as I didn't have any track record in that respect, having simply slipped through the net before then, I think they just dumped me at that school to get me off the truancy register at the secondary school I should have gone to.

I was very sexually aware by that time and I would sometimes go behind the bike sheds with the boys. Apparently it's not uncommon for children with autism to be sexually precocious, not least because they don't understand that certain types of behaviour are inappropriate in a normal social setting. And as they were boys of my age, it was only really what I suppose you would call 'normal' sexual exploration.

So although I did get into trouble for it with the teachers, they didn't seem to be *too* bothered about it. Which was unfortunate, in a way, because it meant that my behaviour didn't raise any particular red flags that might have led to a discussion about why I was acting the way I was. Even so, I'm sure everyone heaved a huge collective sigh of relief when I decided, after a couple of months, that even being sent to the sort of care home described by Mum would be better than being at that school, and I simply stopped going.

Outside of school, I was continuing my 'adult' relationship with Rajan. I was still living at home, but I was independent in many ways by that time and was coming and going more or less as I wanted. I always borrowed Mum's phone whenever I was going into town on my own, and with a phone in my backpack, a boyfriend who was more than twice my age, and a mum who didn't set any boundaries for me, I thought I was all grown-up. I think that was another reason why I couldn't get my head around going to school, particularly a school for children with problems!

Mum met Rajan quite early on in our 'relation-ship'. Her only comment after I had introduced her to the 27-year-old man I was spending all my time with was, 'Aahh. I'm really glad you've got a friend.'

She needed her own space, I suppose. And, to be fair, Mum had problems of her own.

She didn't really know how to look after me and, without any family members other than her cousin Cora to support her, she wasn't coping very well. I used to think it was just me she couldn't cope with – I'm sure it isn't easy trying to look after a child with Asperger syndrome, particularly when you're a single parent on your own. But I realised when I was older that there were many other aspects of life she struggled to deal with. So I can understand how she might have welcomed the opportunity to get a break from me. Perhaps, though, being relieved that her 12-year-old daughter had an adult boyfriend was a step too far, even if that daughter hadn't had the communication and interaction disabilities that handicapped me.

I know Mum felt very guilty about it all. She has always been quick to criticise anyone with children who goes away even for a weekend without them. So she did try to be present in body, if not in spirit. I think she consoled herself, too, with the thought that although I was difficult to deal with, she was doing her job as a mother by not asking anyone else for help. In retrospect, it might have been better if she had.

Mum always told people – including me, on many occasions – that she really *was* doing her best for me and that I had always 'sabotaged' her relationships with my difficult behaviour. I think it was her use of the word sabotaged that particularly upset me, because of its implication of deliberate acts on my behalf. She was certainly very convincing though. I know Cora had looked up Asperger syndrome when I was first diagnosed with it and that she understood the effects it had on me. But even Cora believed that her first loyalty should be to Mum, and she did try to support her in any way she could, despite her own mental-health issues. The result of it all was that, by the time I was 12, I had accepted that I was a badly behaved, inconsiderate and very difficult child who fully deserved to be branded the black sheep of the family.

As I got older, I realised that Mum wasn't really to blame for her rapid mood swings – which I found incredibly stressful – or for any of the other manifestations of the bad experiences she must have had when she was a child. When Mum was about the same age I was when I started seeing Rajan, she was taken into care when her mother got a new partner. She must have felt as though she had been abandoned by the one person in the world who should have put her needs above those of anyone else. It probably also explained what made her think she was doing her best for me, because whatever else Mum did or didn't get right, she didn't ever abandon me, which, in her eyes, was the single worst thing that could possibly happen to a child.

Obviously, because of what had been going on with Tom, I did need the intervention of social services, and Mum needed help too. But, to Mum, asking anyone for help would have meant she had failed. And she couldn't have coped with that. So we stumbled on with our lives, making a terrible mess of it all in our own, individual ways.

Even after I stopped going to school, I wasn't happy. I decided it must be because I was in the wrong relationship. So I decided to drop Rajan and go out with another guy, called Naseer. I think Rajan was relieved when I told him I didn't want to be with him anymore. I had begun to sense that he was getting tired of me, which is what gave me the confidence to start chatting to Naseer and then to break things off with Rajan. I'm pretty sure he would have ditched *me* before too long. So I saved him the trouble and, coincidentally, made his disapproving friends happy too.

Naseer worked in a local kebab shop. He was a bit closer to my age, at 18, good-looking, much taller than most of the other Afghan boys, and quite fair-skinned. He had come to England, from a refugee camp in Afghanistan, as an unaccompanied 14-year-old asylum seeker, hidden in the back of a lorry on a long, arduous and very frightening journey through Iran and Turkey into Europe. When he finally reached the UK, he was looked after for the next four years by a foster family. As a result of coming over at such a relatively young age and going to school here, he spoke good English and had more of an English sense of humour than many of his friends. I was impressed by the stories he told me about his adventures, and by the fact that he had his own car.

We went for a drive on our first date. It was my time of the month and I was wearing a sanitary towel, so I refused to have sex with him in the car as he wanted me to do, although I didn't tell him why. The embarrassment I had felt about having my periods at primary school had left its mark and I would have found it very uncomfortable trying to explain it to him. It didn't require me to have fully functioning emotional radar to be able to pick up on the fact that he was annoyed about it. Afterwards, he told his friends and everyone at the park that I wasn't a girl at all, and for a while they all called me 'Boy' and made fun of me.

Naseer's friends often went with him in his car when he did deliveries for the kebab shop and, after a while, I started to go too. The first time I slid on to the front seat to sit beside him, one of the other men asked me coldly, 'Who do you think you are? Where are you getting these ideas from? Move!' Apparently, I had failed to pick up on the unspoken rule that only girls who were the established girlfriends of specific men were allowed to sit in the front of the car. The girls at the bottom of the pecking order – the younger ones, of 15 and 16, who were passed around amongst Naseer's friends – always sat in the back. I was somewhere between the two, but still definitely a back-seat girl.

Most of the other girls who hung out with Naseer and his friends had grown up on council estates in the area, and although I had a regional accent that wasn't very different from theirs, it was different enough for them to notice. Which meant that, as usual, I didn't fit into any category: to the front-seat girls, I was beneath their contempt and they completely ignored me; to the back-seat girls, I was a snob. I was a bit more popular with the boys, however, I think because I was younger than all the others and they thought I was 'cute'.

One evening, a couple of weeks after our first date, we were all crammed into Naseer's car while he was making his deliveries when he suddenly called over his shoulder to me, 'We're going to stop off at my flat. I want to fuck you.' I was very embarrassed because he had said it so openly, but I was used to being humiliated. So when he pulled up outside his flat, we left the others in the car, smoking weed and listening to music, while we went upstairs.

Naseer was quite gentle and didn't hurt me when we had sex. As soon as he had zipped up his trousers, however, he became irritable and impatient. 'I have deliveries to make,' he snapped at me when I told him I was going to have a quick wash. 'There isn't time for you to wash. Or do *that*.' He scowled at me as I sat on the edge of his bed trying to re-thread the shoelace that had come loose from one of the Doc Martens I always wore.

'It's okay,' I told him quickly. 'I'll take them off. I'll just walk down the stairs in my bare feet.'

'No, keep them on.' He sounded really angry. 'There isn't time for this.'

I am not the most co-ordinated of people at the best of times, and I'm even worse when I'm under pressure. So I stumbled as I followed him down the stairs, even though I was trying really hard not to trip over my shoelaces. When we got to the car, everyone laughed at me, because they knew what we had done and because one of them called me 'a retard' for not tying the laces on my shoes.

Rajan had sometimes pushed me around and often said unkind things to me, but he was never physically violent. Whereas Naseer was volatile and the first man I had been with who made me feel really nervous. He smoked a lot of weed, so his moods could change in the blink of an eye from cheerful to aggressive. It was a trait he shared with many of the other boys who had come to this country from refugee camps. I could always tell which of them had spent their childhood in the camps, because they were the ones who were quick-tempered and unpredictable.

It was often small things that gave it away. For example, if there was ever a sudden loud noise, there would be a split-second when you could see the paralysing fear in their eyes, and then they would go ballistic. They all had different triggers. For some, it was a door slamming or a pan being dropped on the floor. The earliest childhood memories for many of them were of the sound of bombs exploding and of waiting to see where the next one would fall. So it wasn't surprising they reacted the way they did to anything unexpected. They might learn to live with the horrific memories of those childhood experiences, but they wouldn't ever recover completely from the psychological damage that living in the refugee camps had caused.

Most of Naseer's friends could be aggressive, and they were all paranoid about people making fun of them. Several of them were dealing in drugs – mostly weed and sometimes a bit of coke. So they were also paranoid about getting caught. So much so, in fact, that they seemed to believe there were coppers watching them on every street corner. I was with Naseer and his friends on more than one occasion when someone came to do a deal with them and they noticed a stranger glance in their direction as he walked past and beat the crap out of their would-be customer. It was because they thought he had brought someone with him, although I don't know if they were more afraid of getting caught or of being stabbed in the back. So, despite the laughing and joking around, there was always an underlying tension and hostility, which smoking copious amounts of weed didn't really help to control.

During the four years Naseer had lived in England, he had absorbed many aspects of the British way of life. But he still retained some of the more traditional ideas from his own culture that he had grown up with. And because he had very strict views about how women should behave, a lot of the things I did made him angry.

Chapter 6

Naseer hated me showing my teeth when I laughed. The first time he noticed me doing it, his eyes narrowed and seemed to darken until they were almost black. Then he grabbed hold of me with one hand and shoved the fingers of his other hand into my mouth. He did it with so much aggressive force that he scratched the back of my throat and made me gag. He smiled and made a joke out of it afterwards, and although he had really hurt me, I didn't say anything because I didn't want to make a fuss in front of his friends. I knew he was really angry and I was confused about what I had done wrong. After the same thing had happened a few more times, I learned to cover my mouth with my hand whenever I laughed.

Another thing that made Naseer angry was if I used my left hand when I was eating. Muslims use the left hand for doing things like cooking, cleaning and washing themselves after they've been to the loo. Whereas the right hand is reserved for 'clean' activities, like shaking hands and eating. It was a rule I often forgot, and whenever I picked up food with my left hand, he would snatch it and then smack me, hard.

Once, when we were going up in the lift to his flat, I said something that offended him and he banged my head against the metal wall. I hadn't been intentionally rude. I think we had been joking around and I had failed to notice the line that was often invisible to me but always drawn somewhere in the sand that divided joke from insult. His sudden attack took me completely by surprise and I didn't even have time to raise my hands to try to protect my head. Which was probably just as well, because he smashed my head so hard against the wall of the lift that my fingers might have been crushed if they had been in the way. He still slept with me though, when we got inside his flat – on the filthy sheet that always covered his bed and without using a condom. And I still did what he wanted me to do, even though my head was throbbing painfully, because the idea of doing anything else never crossed my mind.

Although Naseer's friends didn't speak much English, I knew when they were making jokes at my expense. They often laughed in my face and called me a retard, which was a word they had learned from the girls who hung out with them. It was a label I accepted, to some extent, because there was no denying in my mind that I was a bit fat and a bit slow. What they didn't realise, however, was that I wasn't slow because I was stupid. It was just that I was afraid of saying anything in case I had misjudged their mood and said something they didn't like. So every time I opened my mouth to speak, I second-guessed myself, thinking, 'I had better not say that. It might be the wrong thing.' Then I would sit there with my mouth open while I ran through in my head all the possible negative consequences of whatever I had been about to say and end up, almost invariably, not saying nothing at all. But because they were the only people in my world, I took it for granted that they were right and that I *was*, if not completely stupid, certainly a bit intellectually inadequate.

They were always doing things to humiliate me and make me look and feel even more dim-witted. And I was always falling into the traps they set for me, like an unwitting participant in some sort of *Groundhog Day*. For example, they would offer me a can of beer, as if they were being casually friendly, and when I drank from it I would get a mouthful of cigarette ends. Or they would hide my shoes, then laugh at me when I searched for them and ask me if I had forgotten where I put them. Or they would open the bathroom when I was on the loo – the lock had been broken during a drunken party at the flat – so that everyone could see me sitting there with my knickers around my ankles.

Naseer often laughed at me too, and sometimes he was quite cruel. Although he had hurt me physically on several occasions, he hadn't ever given me a proper beating. But I knew he was capable of doing it, and I soon learned to switch off my emotions and do whatever he told me to do. So, one day, when he told me to give him a blowjob in the front seat of his car in broad daylight, I slipped automatically into robot mode and didn't even bother to object or try to argue with him. What he knew but I hadn't noticed, however, was that his car was parked right next to a bus full of passengers. Naseer was off his head on speed or coke at the time and he thought it was hilarious when I looked up and saw the expression on the faces of the people sitting on the bus just a few feet away. But I was mortified, and very hurt that he thought it was funny to humiliate me like that.

Mum hadn't ever done anything to build up my confidence, and after spending time with Naseer and his friends, I started to hate myself even more than I had done before. I would sometimes watch the other girls and wonder why they didn't feel intimidated like I did. It was only later that I realised they were probably just better at hiding it. They were certainly better at learning the unspoken rules. Somehow, they were able to back-chat and flirt but always stopped before they got a punch in the mouth. They could obviously read the boys really well, which was something I was totally unable to do, however hard I tried.

Everyone was always laughing and joking around. But if I told a joke, the others would either not react at all because they didn't understand it – sometimes because of the language barrier – or they would take it the wrong way and be angry. On one occasion, the other girls were messing about, calling one of the boys a 'wanker' and accusing another of 'fucking his brother', and everyone was laughing. Then I joined in and called one of them a 'bastard', which, to me, seemed far less insulting than what had already been said. What I didn't know, however, was that the word had a cultural significance to the boys. For a split-second, it seemed as though everyone was holding their breath. Then the boys turned on me, shouting and threatening to kick me out and never speak to me again. It was that sort of thing – which occurred often in one form or another – that made me feel like I was always walking on eggshells with Naseer and with his friends.

Eventually, I learned that it really was better to say nothing at all. As I became used to feeling like the invisible member of their group, I actually turned my head if someone *did* talk to me, to look over my shoulder at the person I expected to see standing behind me who they were actually addressing. I wanted to be with them because I wanted to be with *someone*. But because they didn't seem to see me as another human being like them, I began to feel as though I really wasn't a real person anymore.

I slept at home every night and would get up at about 10 or 11 every morning to go to the park, where I would read my book while I waited for Naseer to wake up and text me to tell me what time to meet him. His flat was in a tower block on a council estate that must have been grim even 50 years ago when it was built. I usually got there at about 5 p.m., so that we could have sex before he went to work. Afterwards, he would turn away from me on to his side and fall instantly asleep. Then I would lie on *my* side, with my back to him, looking out of the window and wondering why I felt even more lonely and empty than I did when I was on my own.

He always woke up in time to go to work a couple of hours later, and I would often go with him. That was how I spent most evenings while I was seeing Naseer, driving round in his car with him and his friends while he did the deliveries for the kebab shop, sometimes stopping off at his flat to have sex again if business was slow. When he finished his shift, at around midnight, he would drop me off near my house and then go out with some of his other friends, the ones I wasn't allowed to meet.

I didn't ever have a key to my house, and as Mum would either still be out or asleep when I got back, she always left a window open for me. There was no bed in my room. So I would slide into Mum's bed, very quietly so that I didn't wake her up if she *had* already come home. Mum always slept facing the wall, with her back to the space she kept for me. If she was awake when I got in, she would talk to me about what she had been doing that day. Then I would tell her lies about my day, how I had gone to the shopping centre in town or to the seaside, where I had bought myself an ice cream. 'What sort of ice cream was it?' she would ask. 'Was it chocolate? That's your favourite, isn't it?' And I would tell her she was right, that it had been chocolate, because I didn't know how to break down the wall that had built up between us and tell her the things I really wanted to say.

I had been seeing Naseer for a few weeks when he met a girl called Lydia, who was 17 and going to college. He put her photograph on the windowsill in his bedroom and often talked about her – how she didn't flirt or sleep around, because she was a 'nice girl' who came from a good family. Whenever he told me about her, he became almost angry with me, which I assumed was because I *wasn't* a 'nice girl' like Lydia was. It made me feel sick with jealousy. I didn't love Naseer, but I did want him – or someone – to love me. I was confused too, because I didn't know how he *did* want me to behave. Sometimes he wanted me to flirt and laugh with his friends, so that he could show me off. And sometimes he got angry and was obviously ashamed of me because I hadn't sat silently in the back of the car.

He often lost his temper and lashed out at me when I didn't keep pace with his ever-changing moods or predict who he wanted me to be at any particular moment. In view of the way he treated me, I feel embarrassed now by the fact that I continued to see him. No one forced me to go to his flat every day. Certainly no one would have cared if I had stopped going. But if I didn't go to Naseer's flat, what would I do instead?

When we moved out of the house with the muddy bathroom floor, Mum had told me to pack up all my things into boxes, which were still piled up in my bedroom at the new house months later, most of them unopened. Although I didn't have a bed, I did have an armchair, and a PlayStation with a couple of games that I played over and over again until they had lost any meaning they might originally have had. It was partly the boredom that got to me. Mostly though, it was the loneliness. And I knew that, without Naseer and his friends, I wouldn't have anyone at all.

What made it worse was that if I was at home, I was more or less confined to my bedroom during the day, because being anywhere else in Mum's pristine showroom of a house wasn't really an option. I was so afraid of making a mess that it didn't feel like *my* home at all. If I ever knocked over a glass of juice or spilled anything else in the living room, Mum would come marching in from the kitchen almost before it reached the floor, snatch up the rug, sigh, march back out again without saying a word and throw it into the washing machine. She would usually look more disappointed than angry, but I did sometimes wonder if she had unusually sensitive hearing, like a bat, or maybe a camera hidden in every room!

It was because of those sorts of incidents that I didn't want even to sit in the house, let alone *do* anything in it that could potentially result in even a temporary stain being made on the immaculate, white sofa or one of the clinically clean work surfaces in the kitchen. So, during the day, before I went to meet Naseer at his flat, I would go out – into the garden or to the park in the summer and, when it was wet or cold, to sit in a cubicle in the public toilets and read my book. Going *somewhere* was better than being at home on my own.

Even when Mum *was* at home during the day, she would be cleaning and/or having rows with me. We always seemed to argue when we were there together during that period of my childhood. Whatever it was that instigated the rows, they usually all ended up the same way, with her accusing me of hating her. 'I always try to do my best for you,' she would tell me, in a voice that somehow managed to convey both anger and self-pity. 'Why do you always have to throw it back in my face?'

Later, after Naseer, when Mum realised what was going on, she asked me, 'What's wrong with you? Why would you prefer to be with those people rather than stay at home with me?' But even if I had wanted to stay at home and face all the arguments, she wasn't actually there most of the time. I sometimes wonder what she thought I was doing, left on my own all day and half the night. She knew I wasn't going to school and that I was coming home after midnight every night. Surely that in itself might have been a clue that *something* wasn't right.

I was still seeing Naseer when I started 'going out' with a 17-year-old Moroccan boy called Karim. Karim had come to England legitimately, on a student visa, not long before I met him, and was studying at college. The other guys I used to hang out with didn't like him, so to avoid their bullying he used to go to a park a bit further out of town, where I sometimes went too, for similar reasons, when I wanted to get away from the others.

There was nothing wrong with Karim. The reason he was picked on was because he seemed to be a bit slow-witted in comparison with Naseer and his friends. A bit like me, in fact. He had a couple of kittens, which he loved to bits. The first time I met him he had brought them with him to the park, and it made me laugh the way they came bounding back as soon as he called them. I think it was partly because of the way he treated them that I knew he wouldn't do me any harm.

He asked if I wanted to go back to his flat with him that first day, and after I had helped him mash up some food for the kittens, I had sex with him. I liked him because he was gentle and kind to me, because he got upset when he found out I was still seeing Naseer, and because he stood up for me when the others teased me and slagged me off. I was impressed, too, by the way he didn't let their taunts put him off doing what he wanted to do. I think it was because I felt safe with him that I lied to Mum and told her I had lost my virginity to him.

There must have been some reason why I chose that particular time to tell Mum I had had sex with someone, but I can't remember what it was. I don't know how I expected her to react to the news that her 12-year-old daughter had lost her virginity – whether it had been to a 17-year-old Moroccan boy or anyone else. Whatever reaction I might have anticipated, I was surprised by her response. 'Aaaah,' she said, smiling at me with an expression of maternal fondness. 'My little girl's all grown-up at last.'

The next day, she made an appointment for me to see the doctor, who asked me if everything was all right. Before I could open my mouth to answer,

Mum spoke for me. 'She's got herself a boyfriend,' she said proudly, as if she was talking about a toddler who had just taken her first steps or used a potty for the first time. 'So we *just* want to make sure she's safe.' The doctor looked at me for a moment with her eyebrows slightly raised. Then she sighed, wrote out a prescription and handed it to Mum.

Every morning after that, Mum would make me a cup of tea and put it on the sideboard in the living room with one of the pills beside it. After she had gone back into the kitchen, I would pick up the pill, crush it between my thumb and index finger, and drop the chalky contraceptive particles into the toilet.

I hated taking tablets of any kind. Perhaps that was partly Mum's influence, from the time she had refused to let me take the tablets that were prescribed for me when I was first diagnosed with Asperger syndrome. But that wasn't the reason why I didn't swallow a single one of the contraceptive pills. It was because I didn't want to face the reality of what I was doing, or of what was being done to me. Naseer hadn't ever used a condom, and Karim didn't either. But in the imaginary world I had built for myself, I wasn't having sex with men, so I couldn't get pregnant.

Taking a contraceptive pill would have challenged the world I wanted to believe I was living in. And if that happened, I would no longer be able to pretend to myself that everything was okay. It seems extraordinary now to think that I projected all the things that worried and distressed me on to that one, small tablet, which Mum had been so proud to obtain for me and which, to me, represented a terrible truth I wasn't equipped to face.

I had started trying to avoid Naseer by that time, although he still had a lot of influence over me. But it wasn't Naseer I was afraid of, despite his mood swings and sometimes aggressive behaviour. It was Karim.

Karim was never physically violent towards me. In fact, he didn't ever treat me badly in any way. On the contrary, he offered me a safe environment and a real relationship. When I went to his flat, we watched TV or listened to music and had dinner together. But although I didn't consciously realise it at the time, I thought the fact that he was offering me all this nice stuff meant that he believed I was a nice person. And that wasn't something my incredibly low self-esteem would allow me to accept. Because if I *was* a nice person, that would mean I didn't deserve what Tom, Rajan and Naseer had done to me. Perversely, I almost *wanted* to be a bad person, because then I didn't have to examine the confused but basically negative image I had of myself.

I don't know if that makes any sense. It's difficult to explain what I mean. It's just that if you've got no one else in the world, it's very scary to think that the people you *do* know might not actually care about you, or might even want to harm you. Instead of believing that all those people are bad, it's easier to blame yourself: if they're good, I must be the one that isn't, and that's okay, because at least it means they don't want to hurt me, so I don't have to be afraid of them. And as well as blaming myself, I blamed Karim too, for trying to 'control' me by wanting to keep me safe.

The only people I ever talked to at that time were people I couldn't really communicate with, because of the language barrier that existed between us. I had no one I could discuss things with, and no one who would have believed me if I had. I was frightened of losing the people I *did* have, so I became the person I thought they wanted me to be. I was always acting a role, going where I was told to go, doing what I was told to do. I was 12 years old and had had virtually no intellectual or moral guidance at all, except what I picked up in the books I read so voraciously. I didn't know what I wanted or even what I was thinking, and I was always afraid of saying the wrong thing. So it was easier to shut down and wait for someone else to tell me what to do, what to think and what to say.

When Karim was gentle and kind to me, I began to feel like a real person again. That should have been a good thing. But it was actually something I couldn't allow to happen, because if I became a real person, with thoughts, ideas and aspirations of my own, I would have to confront and deal with the realities of my life. I didn't understand any of that consciously at the time, of course. I didn't know why I made the decision to stop seeing the one person who really did care about me.

Karim knew when I first met him that I was going out with Naseer. It was the sort of town where everyone seemed to know everyone else's business, particularly the people who used to hang out in the park and outside the kebab shops. I think Karim thought he would be able to win me away from Naseer simply by being nice to me. It makes sense, on the face of it: if you're a nice person and you treat a girl well, it would be natural to expect her to leave the horrible person she's with so that she could be with you.

When Karim suggested that I should stop seeing Naseer and just go out with him, I did tell him that I would. But after he had seen me a couple of times outside the kebab shop with Naseer, he realised that I had lied and one evening he asked me why I kept going back to someone who treated me so badly. I didn't have an answer to his question. I didn't even want to think about what the answer might be. So I began to avoid him. One of the negative things about having a good visual memory is that I can still remember very clearly the expression on his face the first time I saw him in town after that and refused to speak to him.

I had been seeing Karim for about a month when I stopped answering his calls. I felt really bad about hurting him, but at least I knew who I was again. Perhaps some of his thoughtfulness had rubbed off on me though, because I was starting to think that I had had enough of Naseer's aggression and of being constantly humiliated by him.

One of Naseer's friends was an Afghan called Saleem, who was always really nice to me. He didn't ever say anything when the others were taunting and embarrassing me, but he often put his arm around my shoulders afterwards and asked, 'Are you all right?' I was grateful for his kindness, particularly when I was feeling bad about the way I was treating Karim and anxious about how I was going to get away from Naseer.

At the top of the hierarchy that existed amongst the girls were the established girlfriends. Next were the girls who slept with just one or two of the guys. At the bottom were the girls who had sex with anyone who asked. When the others found out that I was spending time with Saleem, they made what I suppose was the obvious assumption, and I dropped further down the pecking order. They were wrong though, to begin with, because although I did start going to Saleem's flat, we just played *Grand Theft Auto* and he didn't try to have sex with me.

Saleem had a lot of Polish and other European friends, who he often invited round to his flat for parties. I had already started drinking alcopops by that time, but when he started asking me to his parties too, I drank vodka. I felt safe with Saleem, and comfortable with his friends, who weren't aggressive and critical if I drank a bit too much and got mouthy or laughed too loudly. I felt as though I could relax when I was at his flat and I loved going there. At least, I did to begin with.

Chapter 7

Saleem and his friends slept during the day. So I would go down to his flat in the evenings. It was a studio flat and if you wanted to talk to anyone when there was a party in full swing, you had to shout to be heard above the thud of the music. One night, one of the Polish guys put his mouth close to my ear and bellowed, 'I want to talk to you. Let's go in there.' He nodded his head towards the bathroom.

I was really drunk, so when he locked the bathroom door behind us, then grabbed me by the throat and slammed me up against the door, it took a few seconds for me to realise what he was doing.

'It's okay,' I told him, gagging and trying to turn my head away from the stench of his breath. 'I'll give you what you want. Just put me down.'

I don't know if he even heard me, because he was already shouting at me, saying something slurred and angry that I didn't understand. He was a huge, bull-dog of a man, who didn't flinch when I slapped him. I don't think he even felt it.

'It's okay,' I said again, more loudly this time. 'I'll give you what you want.' And that's when it dawned on me that he didn't want me to *give* it to him; he wanted to take it.

Suddenly, for no apparent reason, he bashed my head against the door. Then he released his grip on my throat and spun me round, so that I was facing away from him. Despite the fact that he was standing very close behind me, I somehow managed to swing my leg and kick the door. I kept on kicking it and screaming so loudly I could probably be heard at the end of the street. But instead of anyone coming to help me, someone in the other room turned up the music, and I knew I was screwed.

Until that moment, I had always believed that, ultimately, I was the one who was in control of the things that happened to me. Saleem, particularly, made me feel that way, because he made me feel safe. So I thought I had been making my own choices. Admittedly, many of them weren't good ones and I often did things – or allowed them to be done to me

– because I didn't know how to say no. But I had never really felt coerced into doing anything I didn't want to do. Now, though, I realised that I was completely at the mercy of the Polish guy who was pinning me against the door with one hand while unzipping his trousers with the other.

I knew there was no point trying to fight him. He was more than twice my size, in every dimension, and at least four times stronger. If I did try to resist, there was a very distinct possibility that I would simply end up with broken bones, maybe even a shattered nose, and he would take what he wanted anyway.

I had stopped struggling and was trying to detach my mind from what was about to happen to me when there was an almighty bang on the door. The wall on either side of it seemed to vibrate and I could hear someone shouting. In fact, it was more like a roar than a shout and I couldn't make out what he was saying. Then the bathroom door splintered and I fell back against the basin just as a man burst into the room.

While the others had turned up the volume of the music to drown out my cries for help, just one man had come to my rescue and prevented me from being raped. Eddie was a six-foot-tall, disabled, speech-impaired Eastern European guy who wore a large, old-fashioned hearing aid and who Saleem and his friends treated like a sort of mascot. Even the drunken Polish guy could see that he was in the kind of rage that would have made it extremely inadvisable to try to argue or reason with him. So he snatched up his phone from where it had dropped on to the floor and fled without a word.

A few minutes later, when things had calmed down a bit and I was sitting in the living room, still in a state of shock, I realised that it wasn't *his* phone the Polish guy had taken; it was mine. Someone had turned off the music by that time and they had all stopped drinking, and when I told Saleem what had happened with my phone, I noticed several of the other men glance at him anxiously.

'We have got to get it back,' Saleem told me. 'Come on, you must come with me.' The last thing I wanted to do was see my attacker again. But Saleem sounded impatient, almost angry, and I knew his 'invitation' wasn't optional.

A couple of the other guys came with us too. But no one spoke as we ran down the stairs of the house and out into the street. We caught up with the Polish guy a short distance down the road. He spun round when Saleem called out his name and, for a moment, looked quite scared. When Saleem told him why we had followed him, he barely glanced at my phone before handing it over.

Afterwards, the other guys laughed at Eddie – although that was nothing new, as everyone always did. They didn't talk specifically about what had happened though, either then or at any other time. But, as I far as I was aware, Saleem didn't ever invite the Polish guy to his flat again.

Perhaps it was because no one ever mentioned the incident that I didn't really wonder why Saleem had been so anxious to get my phone back for me. If I had thought about it, I suppose I would just have assumed that he was being nice, watching out for me – although that didn't really square with the fact that neither he nor anyone else, except Eddie, had come to my aid when I was about to be raped. It wasn't until later that I realised his only concern had been for himself, because I had often dialled his phone number from my phone, and because he couldn't be certain that I wouldn't report it as stolen to the police.

In fact, I was still using Mum's phone at that time. She would give it to me when I went into town, and if I needed her for any reason, I would call her friend Derek, who ran the charity shop where she used to help out during the day. Coincidentally, it wasn't long after the incident at Saleem's flat that Derek bought me a phone of my own. I think he got fed up with not being able to contact Mum when he wanted to. He would top up the credit on my new phone from time to time too, and when it ran out, I would just wait for Saleem to call me.

It was actually Mum who got me involved with Saleem in the first place. She had no idea who he was or what it would lead to, of course. I suppose she was just trying to be helpful, now that her little girl had lost her virginity and was 'all grown-up'.

Saleem was 25, slim, with long, pianist's fingers and creamy, light-brown skin. I liked the look of him the first time I saw him. And one evening, when I had climbed in through the open window after getting home later than Mum, I told her about him while we were chatting in her bed. 'I know which road he lives in,' I said. 'But I don't know which house.'

I don't think she asked me what had happened to Karim – the boy she believed had been responsible for transforming me from girl to 12-year-old woman. She didn't really say anything very much about what I had told her, but the next day she went to the road I had mentioned and knocked on every door, asking any man who opened one, 'Are you Saleem?'

When someone finally said 'Yes', she told him, simply, 'My daughter fancies you.'

'He seemed very well-mannered,' she told me a couple of days later, when she was driving me down his street in her car prior to dropping me off outside his house. 'It's nice for you to have a friend.'

I was still seeing Naseer at that time, although I stopped when, in my mind, the relationship between me and Saleem had become real and exclusive. Even then, Saleem made sure I understood that he didn't want anyone to know about 'us'. 'Don't spread it around,' he told me. 'Just keep it between us.' So whenever Naseer called in at Saleem's flat while I was there during the day, playing computer games, Saleem hid me in a cupboard and told me to keep very quiet until his visitor had gone. Sometimes, Naseer stayed for what seemed like hours, but was probably only one or two. When he finally left, Saleem would smile at me as he opened the cupboard door to let me out of my hiding place, and I would feel proud because I knew he was pleased with me.

I believed everything Saleem told me and I wanted him to know that he could trust me and rely on me. It wasn't until much later that I realised that Naseer always knew I was there on those occasions. Shutting me in the cupboard had been a test, to see if I could keep a secret – even from someone I believed I had been close to – and whether, if pushed too far, I would become impatient and refuse to do what I had been told.

That was why Saleem had been in such a panic when the Polish guy accidentally took my phone. He hadn't had a chance to test me by that time and he must have been afraid in case I got any ideas about reporting my phone as having been stolen, or even telling the police what had happened in the bathroom at his flat. When you're a pimp, the last thing you want is for the police to find out that you have any link to a 12-year-old girl.

For a while, I thought Saleem and I were very close. Having sex with him was different from the way it was with Naseer, not least because he always cuddled me afterwards. Then we would watch television together and he would offer me weed, which I hadn't ever smoked before then. I really did believe that I was his girlfriend and that he cared about me and liked having me around. And then other men started coming to his flat while I was there.

What had happened with the Polish guy had really frightened me. Before that day, I had believed that if I hit a man hard enough, I would be able to fight him off, however big or strong he was. So it had come as quite a shock to me to realise that even though I had hit the Polish guy with all my strength, he hadn't even blinked. I had been naive before that incident. After it I felt very weak and vulnerable.

A couple of days later, Naseer turned up at Saleem's flat while I was there. I hadn't had sex with anyone since the day the Polish guy tried to rape me, and I wouldn't have wanted Naseer to touch me even if Saleem hadn't been there. But because I didn't want to argue with him and make a scene, I went along with it when Naseer pulled me over to the bed and had sex with me, just a few feet away from where Saleem was sitting on the sofa, watching TV as if nothing was happening.

I can remember quite clearly lying there with Naseer on top of me, looking up at the cracks in the ceiling above my head and thinking, 'I don't want this. It was meant to be better than this.' Until that moment, I had always been emotionally numb. Having sex with Naseer while the man I believed cared about me sat in the same room, placid and indifferent, suddenly made me feel incredibly sad.

The following evening, Naseer came round to Saleem's flat again. This time though, neither of them paid me any attention. They sat together, watching television and smoking weed, and when I tried to cuddle Saleem he pushed me away. Later that night, Naseer drove me home to Mum's house without speaking to me.

Although Saleem was still polite and kind to me, and always bought me food when I was hungry, he didn't ever want to be intimate with me again after that. I thought I had messed up. I thought it was my fault I wasn't living 'the dream' I saw other, older girls living, the ones who had monogamous relationships with real boyfriends and who were at all the parties, drinking and having a good time. But the reality was that I wasn't one of the girlfriends, and I never would be.

When I went back to Saleem's flat the next night – like a lamb to the slaughter – Naseer was there again, this time with a guy whose face I recognised but who I hadn't ever spoken to. The three men talked and smoked weed while I sat on the bed. Then the guy I didn't know came and sat down beside me, took off his shoes, put his arm around me and started kissing my neck. Saleem and Naseer were watching us, and although my whole body had tensed, I didn't try to push him away, or resist when he thrust me down on the bed, pulled off his trousers and had sex with me. Inside my head, someone was shouting

'No!' But, for some reason, I couldn't make the word come out of my mouth.

When he had finished, he put his trousers on again, walked over to the sofa, took the spliff Saleem held out to him and sat down on the battered armchair to watch television, as though nothing had happened.

That's when the truth finally dawned on me: I hadn't been invited to the parties because I was Saleem's girlfriend, or even part of the group; I was at his flat to work. The 15-year-olds and 16-year-olds had been used and abused so many times that they had begun to lose their appeal. So I was the new attraction, a younger girl for Saleem's friends and acquaintances to have sex with. By not making a fuss or going to the police after the Polish guy tried to rape me, and by hiding for so long in the cupboard in Saleem's flat when he told me he didn't want Naseer to know I was there, I had passed the test and proved that I wasn't going to be a threat to the system Saleem was running.

I was going to Saleem's flat almost every day, having sex with whoever he had invited there for that purpose. I knew there wasn't any point trying to fight it. And, in the greater scheme of things, what did it really matter? The bruises and bite marks would heal. I just had to keep telling myself that it wasn't *that* bad. I had already sunk as low as it was possible to go, so at least they couldn't do any worse to me. I was wrong about that, as it turned out. Having accepted what I believed was the inevitable, I began to drink quite heavily, and then things *did* get much worse.

It was while I was at the park one afternoon that I met someone I really liked. Atif was 17, short and chubby, and really, really nice. He was an asylum seeker from Afghanistan who shared a house in the countryside with a couple of his friends, not far from where Mum and I lived. He was genuinely unlike all the others, and meeting him made me feel excited, the way children feel when something good is about to happen.

A couple of days after we first met, Atif sent me a text asking me to go round to his house. At least, I thought the text had come from him. But when I got there he was out and his friend asked me to have sex with him. I was so used to it by that time that I didn't even consider the possibility of saying no. I just took off my trousers and lay down on the sofa, like some sort of robot that can't think for itself and has been programmed to obey.

Later that evening, when Atif came home, he cooked dinner for me, then we sat together on the sofa with our arms around each other and watched TV. He knew I had slept with his friend – and, later, that I did so again, on several other occasions – and *I* knew he hated it. But he didn't know what to do about it, any more than I did.

Atif worked very long hours in a kebab shop – a different one from the one Naseer did deliveries for. So I didn't see him as much as I would have liked to. Whenever we did see each other, he was always gentle and nice to me. Eventually, I began to tell him a bit about some of the things that were happening to me at Saleem's flat, where I was still having sex with Naseer and a number of his friends. I didn't tell Atif that I was being raped, but I did confide in him that I was scared of Saleem and his friends and that the only reason I went back there every day was because I didn't know how to get out of it.

I could see that he was upset, even by the small amount I told him. 'I will protect you,' he used to say, even though he probably knew as well as I did that he couldn't. 'I want to be with you,' he told me. 'I want us to have a baby.'

When I did fall pregnant – for the first time, amazingly, considering that very few of the men I slept with used condoms – Atif insisted that we must keep the baby when it was born and make a life for ourselves together, as a family. He knew how old I was. But it's normal for girls in Afghanistan to have babies at a much younger age than would be considered acceptable here. The problem was, I couldn't be certain that this baby was Atif's.

I didn't tell anyone else that I was pregnant, not least because I wasn't even certain that I *was*, particularly as I was finding it increasingly difficult to know what was real and what was only happening inside my head. In fact, I tried to avoid thinking about it at all, because doing so just raised questions I couldn't answer. Questions like, were Atif and I really going to live together and bring up our child in a house in the country? Or was that just a fantasy born of a desperate wish for it to be true?

When I started being sick and couldn't bear the thought of eating anything, Saleem knew immediately what was wrong. Perhaps it's the sort of thing you *need* to know when you're a pimp. And perhaps it was the reason why he got me so drunk on vodka one night that I blacked out. I don't suppose my half-starved, super-stressed, 12-year-old body had a strong enough grip on an embryonic child to have been able to hold on to it when the alcohol began to

flood my veins, and I started bleeding the next day
– as I am sure Saleem knew I would.

When I told Atif that I had made a mistake and
hadn't been pregnant after all, he was devastated. We
were sitting side by side in his bed when I told him,
and we both cried. For Atif, the emotion was genuine, because there wasn't going to be a baby after all,
and because he thought I had lied to him when I told
him that there was. For me, crying was what I *thought*
I should be doing in the circumstances. Whereas
what I really felt was detached, as if I was hovering
above my body, watching myself going through the
motions of normal reactions, while not actually feeling anything at all.

Atif did his best to keep me away from the others.
He would buy me little presents, take me out to
dinner and do whatever else he could think of to
persuade me not to go back to Saleem's flat again.
But it seemed that I was programmed to self-destruct,
and to do whatever Saleem told me to do without
thinking about it at all. It scares me when I remember
it now, the way I just switched off and almost colluded
in the terrible damage that was being done to me.
Atif was offering me a genuinely loving relationship,
which was the one thing I had always longed to have.
Yet not only was I going to Saleem's flat almost every

day, I had also started seeing another Afghan asylum seeker, a good friend of Atif called Rahim.

By this time, I was no longer confused about my own self-worth: I hated myself. I didn't feel any anger towards the men who used and abused me every day. I was only angry with myself. I had broken Karim's heart and now I was breaking Atif's. I knew what I was doing to them was wrong. They were both good men and it was an incredibly unkind way to treat them – and possibly an even more unkind way to treat myself. But I didn't seem to be able to do the right thing. I thought I deserved all the violence and aggression I was experiencing, because I deserved to be punished for what I had done to the people I *did* care about.

In a way, Rahim was part of my self-inflicted punishment, because I loathed him. He was in his thirties, an excellent cook and really quite a nice person. But, for some reason, he made my skin crawl. The only person I wanted to be with was Atif. But that wasn't possible because I didn't deserve to be with someone good and kind. In fact, I was so emotionally numb by that time that kindness didn't make me *feel* anything. I had even become indifferent to being constantly ridiculed and humiliated by

Naseer. The only emotions I did still seem to be able to experience were the almost tangible disgust and dislike I felt for Rahim. In some strange way, it was as if I needed to spend time with him to remind myself what it was like to feel *something*.

Rahim worked in the mornings and was free in the afternoons, when everyone else was busy. And it was while I was seeing him that Naseer started taking me to another house, where I learned that the worst can always get worse.

One day when I went to Saleem's flat, Naseer told me, 'There are some boys I want you to see.' I didn't know where he was taking me or what to expect when we got there, although I suppose I must have had some idea, because of what was already happening with Saleem, Naseer and their friends, and with Rahim.

When we got to the house, we sat in the lounge with a couple of other guys, listening to music and drinking. Then Naseer told me to go upstairs. I assumed he was going to come up with me, which he did, but followed by the two other guys. When he took me back to the same house the next day, there were more men drinking in the living room, and by the time I went up to the bedroom, a queue was already forming on the stairs.

Every night followed the same pattern after that: I was given some drinks downstairs and then sent up to the bedroom before everyone else arrived and the real party began. I don't know how many men lined up that first time, or on any of the other nights. Naseer always put a bottle of vodka for me on the bedside table, together with some wet wipes and tissues, and as each man left the bedroom, I just had time to take a swig from the bottle and clean myself up a bit before the door opened again and the next man came in.

A few of them were obviously embarrassed by what they were doing; some even apologised or ruffled my hair and kissed my forehead afterwards. They were the ones I remembered, the ones whose faces I might have been able to pick out from a crowd. But most of them didn't speak to me at all and I barely noticed what they looked like, or how many of them came into the bedroom each night, although I think it was always between five and twelve.

The next time I missed a period, I *knew* I was pregnant. At almost 13, there would have been no other reason why my boobs suddenly got bigger and heavier or why a small but pronounced bump began to develop in my belly. A few of the guys who lined up on the stairs each night used condoms, but many of them didn't. It was their choice. So, sooner or later, it was bound to happen.

I was still seeing Atif at that time, and Rahim too. But I didn't tell *anyone*. I was too frightened to go to the doctor, because I thought that, because of my age, I would be forced to have an abortion, and then social services would get involved. After what Mum had told me about her own experiences as a child in care, I was even more afraid of social services than I was of doctors. So I decided that if I held out for long enough, until it was too late to have an abortion, perhaps they would have to allow me to keep the baby.

I knew a couple of young mums – who were older than me, but can't have been more than 16 – who were in a mother-and-baby unit that sounded like a relatively nice place to be. If I could hide my condition for long enough, perhaps I could go to one too, and then I would be safe. I suppose I saw having a baby as a way out. If I was in a unit like the one the other girls described, Saleem and Naseer couldn't get at me, and if I got the help I needed, I might be able to make a new start. It wasn't just self-interest that prompted my actions: I wanted to have the baby for its own sake too, because I wanted to look after it, to make sure it had a happy childhood and knew it was loved. Giving my child the childhood I wished I had had would seem like another way of starting again.

One day when I went to Atif's house, only Rahim was there. He assumed we were going to have sex, and when I answered him back and refused to sleep with him, he pushed me down the stairs. It happened without any warning and I was so taken by surprise, I couldn't do anything to save myself from tumbling all the way to the bottom. I lay there for a few seconds, too stunned to feel much pain. Then I stood up, and as I did so, I could feel blood pouring down my legs.

I don't know whether Rahim realised what had happened. He probably just thought I was having a massive nosebleed. But he wasn't concerned for me at all. He was just angry, because I had bled all over the carpet in what was a rented flat. At least he let me use the shower though, after he had made me scrub the stain with bleach. I knew then that I could forget about any idea I had had of using the baby as a means of escape and erasing the past. As I stood watching the pale remnants of what might have been disappear into the drains, a voice in my head kept repeating, 'There is no way out for you now.'

Chapter 8

I had had two miscarriages before I turned 13. Not long after the second one, I met a guy at a party at one of the houses who started taking me to different places. I didn't know the word pimp then, but I knew what he was. You could always tell: the pimps were the ones who bought you food and alcohol and were really nice to you. Not because they liked you, as you wanted to believe, but because they saw you as potential profit and were trying to make sure you stuck around.

I had accepted that that was my life by that point. For a very brief period, I even started to enjoy it. That isn't the right word: what I was doing wasn't something anyone could ever *enjoy*. But I don't know how else to describe the positive feeling I had of having been accepted at last. I would go to the parties and tell myself, 'This is where I *want* to be.' And for a child who had never been able to make friends or socialise, I was more than willing to fool myself into believing that I had friends now.

I was going to a lot of parties and drinking very heavily. Sometimes, whole days would pass without my being able to remember anything about them. I still don't know what I did during those lost days. Fortunately though, I always woke up at home the next morning. So someone must have put me in a car every night and driven me there. And however drunk I was, I seemed to have managed to climb in through the window Mum still left open for me.

There was no hot water at most of the houses I went to. I would try to boil a kettle to have a wash, but they used to make green tea in their kettles and it was almost impossible to get them clean. Even when I managed to rinse one out so that the water I poured into the basin wasn't cloudy and discoloured, I had no soap or flannel to wash with. Being clean really mattered to me. In fact, it was the only reason I went home at all a lot of the time. Otherwise, I would probably just have slept on a couch somewhere.

Sometimes, by the time I woke up in the morning, Mum would already have put my dirty clothes through the washing machine and hung them on the line to dry. But mostly I did it. If I was really drunk, I would wait until the next morning to have a bath, although sometimes I misjudged it and woke up lying in freezing cold water with my head only just above the surface.

There was rarely much food at home at that time. I think Mum's attitude was that if I wasn't going to act like a daughter and spend time with her, she wasn't going to act like a mother and provide me with food. She only ate once a day anyway – usually a sandwich made for her by Sid or Derek – and she didn't ever cook for herself. So as I began to stay away from the house more longer periods at a time, she gradually bought less and less food, until there was normally nothing for me to eat at all except the remains of a loaf of bread in the fridge.

By the time I woke up in the mornings, Mum had usually already cleaned the house, got dressed and gone out, either to help at the charity shop or to see friends. Our pristine house wasn't for living in – even by Mum, except briefly, on the occasions when Sid dropped by and she made him a cup of tea. But not wanting to mess up the house wasn't the only reason she didn't stay at home: Mum hated being on her own. She used to say that it was my fault she was forced out, because I was never there, although I realise now that she wouldn't have stayed in just for me anyway. By the time I was 12, we were already leading very separate lives and there was little common ground between us.

I had always appreciated anything Mum did do for me, because I had known from a young age that I was incredibly difficult to deal with and take care of. So I considered myself very lucky when she still took me out for the day sometimes, before things got really bad for me. We would go to the seaside or to Derek's charity shop to help out there and have lunch with him. But that all stopped when I started drinking heavily, not least because I didn't want to go anywhere I couldn't get drunk. After that, Mum did her thing, I did mine, and our paths only ever crossed at all because home was the one place I had access to a constant supply of hot water and electricity.

It was more than an hour's walk from town to where we lived, and as most of it was through the countryside, where there weren't any street lights, it wasn't an easy journey at night. When I was sober enough, I caught the bus to the nearest bus stop and then walked from there to our house, about five minutes away along a dark lane. But the last bus left town before midnight and when I missed it, as I quite often did, I phoned Mum's friend Sid.

I don't know what would have happened to me if it hadn't been for Sid. His number was the most dialled number on my phone. Even when I was so drunk that I had no memory of walking to the bus stop in town from wherever the party had been that night, I somehow always managed to call Sid. It was often at one or two o'clock in the morning and usually at weekends, which is when there were more people at the parties and no one wanted to be bothered with taking me home. I would slur something incoherent down the phone and Sid would say, 'Just stay where you are. I'm coming to pick you up.' His house was about an hour's drive on the other side of town from where I hung out. So I would sit in the darkness at the bus stop, slipping in and out of consciousness, until he arrived to take me home.

I was usually too drunk to be aware of the risk I was taking, sitting alone in the middle of town in the early hours of the morning in an alcohol-fuelled stupor. In fact, I think I was too indifferent to my own well-being by that stage to have been worried if I had realised how foolish it was. Fortunately, Sid was more conscious of the risks and more concerned for my safety.

He was a lot older than Mum – in his sixties at least – and although he was always nice to me, he would be really angry with her on the nights when he took me home, laying into her for not knowing where I had been or who I had been with. Mum would just sigh and respond in the way she always did when anyone even hinted at the possibility that she might be underplaying her role as mother, by saying words to the effect of, 'You have no idea what a heavy burden I have to carry.'

It was because of the furious rows Sid had with Mum that I always used to walk to the bus stop in town before I phoned him, rather than calling him from whichever house the party had been held at that night. If he was as angry as that with Mum, I certainly didn't want to risk him going back to the party house later and kicking someone's head in. After a while, he started inviting me and Mum to his house for lunch and then taking us to the seaside for the afternoon. I think he did it to include me in something a family might do, and because he didn't know how else to deal with the situation.

I don't suppose he could have imagined what the true situation really was. He just knew that someone must be paying for me to get drunk and that, as I was only 12 or 13 years old, it wasn't someone of my own age. I suppose he knew, too, that some form of payback was likely to be expected.

Sid had seen the bruises that always covered my body. Sometimes they were accidental, caused, for example, when I was being taken from one party to another and was too drunk to notice that I had cracked my head as I was being pushed into a car. More often they were inflicted on me deliberately by violent men during sex.

Sid's instinct was to try to protect me and keep me safe, but I don't think he had any idea how bad things really were.

There were a couple of much older girls – in their twenties – who were around at that time and who were both serious heroin addicts. The bruises on their arms were the visible signs that they had sunk as low as it's possible to go. And although I wasn't using heroin, I was down there with them, at the bottom of the pile. I was as faceless to the men who had sex with me as most of them were to me. Despite everything, however, I still told myself I was having a good time, that it was fun to go to parties at different houses and to be in the company of other people, even if none of them ever spoke directly to me.

Somewhere along the way, Atif had simply melted into the background. He hadn't been able to protect me or keep me away from other men. So I didn't blame him for giving up on me.

There was a house about a 20-minute walk from ours that I started going to on my own after one of the pimps had taken me there on the first occasion. It was one of a couple of houses I went to by myself, because it was close to home and because the three guys who lived there were nice to me, although what 'being nice to me' meant by that stage was giving me a cuddle and some vodka after they had all had sex with me together. It's sad to think that's all it took to comfort me – a few kind words and as much alcohol as I could drink.

When I was just coming up for 13, they told me they were going to take me to a New Year's Eve party. Because they didn't want their neighbours to see me hanging around outside their house, I wasn't ever allowed to go there unless one of them was going to be at home to let me in. So they always picked me up from the park, which is where I waited for them that evening, all dressed up and excited about being taken to a party.

When they didn't arrive at the time they said they would be there, I phoned one of them, who told me, 'We're coming. We'll be five minutes.' I rang him again 20 minutes later, and a few more times after that. But by midnight they had all turned off their phones. So I saw the New Year in sitting alone on a park bench feeling stupid because I had finally realised that it was just some sort of joke and they hadn't ever intended to take me to a party at all.

It wasn't generally cash that changed hands between the pimps and the men who used me. Most of them had come to England from Afghanistan, or via refugee camps in places like Pakistan, and except for the small number who worked legitimately, they didn't have any money. Some had come into the country illegally, or had outstayed student visas; some were working for £20 a day in kitchens or washing cars, and a few earned a bit more than that working as mechanics. Some of the men who didn't have any money at all would borrow £30 from whoever would lend it to them, buy a bag of weed, sell it for £40, pay back the £30 they had borrowed and spend the £10 profit on weed for themselves.

The one thing they did all seem to be able to find the money for was the quite convincing counterfeit Nike trainers that were sold at the local market for knock-down prices. For some reason, a good pair of (fake) trainers was considered to be one of life's necessities. For most of the men though, it was a hand-to-mouth existence. So the currency that was exchanged for sex with me, or with one of the other girls, was usually a bag of weed, a bottle of vodka or a favour – for example, letting someone stay at your house for a couple of nights.

Some of the guys had already been refused permission to remain in the UK and were trying to keep out of sight of the police, to avoid being deported. Occasionally, I heard that police had raided a mechanics shop or one of the houses where I used to hang out and that they had picked up five or six illegal immigrants. The men already saw the police as the enemy and those raids cemented the animosity they felt towards them. In fact, during one search of a third-floor flat, a guy was so desperate to get away he jumped out of the window and ended up in hospital with several broken bones. Fortunately, I was never around when that sort of thing happened.

The odd thing about it was that however badly some of the boys treated me and the other girls, it felt like 'us and them': we were always on their side when it came to any dealings with the authorities. There were a lot of gangs in the area and they were constantly fighting amongst themselves. They didn't ever involve anyone outside their own community in the fights. Quite a lot of the trouble that occurred – the drug dealing and knife attacks – was due to the

Afghans. So there was a lot of hostility, amongst the Afghans themselves, between them and the police, and towards them from the local indigenous population.

The police didn't like us girls any more than they liked the men. I remember one night we were all standing outside a kebab shop drinking when a couple of police officers started shouting at us. It was about 11 o'clock and I was pretty drunk, so my memory of what happened is a bit hazy, although I do remember the police telling us to move on or they would arrest us. I can see why they thought we were all troublemakers. But if they had bothered to take a closer look, they might have noticed that some of the girls were quite young to be hanging around on street corners in the middle of the night with a group of men. I think the police are better at that sort of thing now; they're more aware of what might be going on under the surface and, in many cases, more willing to try to deal with it. But at the time they just lumped us all together as 'trouble'.

I didn't have any money of my own – not even enough for a bus fare – so I was always hungry. In fact, one of the reasons I got involved with the group of people who used to hang around in town was because they gave me food to eat. I was drinking so heavily by that time that Mum no longer left a cup of tea and a contraceptive pill in the living room for me in the mornings. She left me a can of cider. The only other way I could buy alcohol for myself was if one of the guys who had queued on the stairs at a party house left a tenner on the bedside table and I managed to pocket it before the pimp saw it.

I was given as much free booze as I wanted at the parties, so I drank vodka. But otherwise it was cider. Ten pounds would buy me two or three days' supply of cans of White Ace, which is strong, cheap and drunk by many young teenagers and the homeless. I always spent any money I had on alcohol rather than food. So it wasn't long before I had lost loads of weight and became really thin.

I think Mum was so relieved to have me out of the house every day she probably didn't give much thought to what it was that was luring me away. She obviously knew I was drinking though, or she wouldn't have replaced my morning cup of tea with cider. But, to be fair, I don't think she knew what to do with me.

We still occasionally had our night-time chats and during one of them I told her about the three guys whose house I used to visit and said that I was sleeping with them. I said it in a jokey way – 'One of them is so tall I have to stand on a bucket to do it with him' – and although she laughed, she must have known that I was actually having sex with them.

I liked having those chats with Mum, although they didn't happen very often by that time. It was good to have *someone* to talk to, even if I didn't ever say the things I probably should have said. I always toned down what I told her about the parties, letting her believe that it was just one guy a night. In fact, whenever I told her anything significant, I always made it into a joke, laughing and saying things like, 'I got really drunk last night and went home with this guy and when I woke up this morning I realised he was really gross.' I did it because Mum was quite prudish about sex and didn't talk openly about it, and because I knew she believed that anything bad that happens to a woman in relation to sex is always her own fault – whether she's drunk or just 12 or 13 years old and not really a woman at all.

Mum didn't ever use the word sex, so I didn't either. When I was telling her about my exploits, I would make her laugh by talking about 'doing it'. Then she would share some funny anecdote of her own, telling me, for example, 'I went on a date with this guy and he tried to make me put my hand down his trousers. So I told him, "I am *not* touching *that* thing".' I liked it when we had conversations like that, because it made it seem as though we were two girlfriends joking around and gossiping.

I suppose Mum decided to tell herself that I had friends and was happy, and not think about what it was I was actually doing. With me out of the way, she was able to live her life the way she wanted to live it, without all the arguments and physical fights that had been such an integral part of my childhood for the previous few years. But the fact that she was amused by what I told her and didn't ever try to stop me going out, even when Sid got really angry with her, made me believe that what was happening was normal and okay.

I think it was to help make herself feel better about it all that Mum took me shopping for new clothes occasionally. All my clothes were cheap – either bought at the market for £3 or £4 or picked out from a bag of adults' clothes at Derek's charity shop – and most were the sort of thing a stereotypical prostitute might wear.

I still wore long skirts or trousers almost all the time – although it might sound like an odd thing to say in view of the life I was leading, I didn't feel safe in short skirts. My favourite maxi skirt was made of black velvet decorated with swirls of sequins. I used to wear it with one of the several similar tops I had, which were either red or blue and quite low-cut with very thin straps. I always wore high heels, never flats, and carried a small, brightly coloured backpack stuffed to bursting with all my bits and pieces, including at least one book and a bottle of cheap perfume.

Sometimes, one of the pimps, or one of the other men, would tell me they were going to take me out for a meal or to the cinema. It never happened, of course, but I still got up every morning thinking, 'Today might be the day when I get taken somewhere special.' So I always got dressed up, just in case, and then spent the day pretending to myself that I actually was going to go somewhere special that night, perhaps to the sort of party where I would stay downstairs, drinking and chatting with everyone else.

For about six months, every day followed more or less the same pattern. I would drink a can of cider as soon as I woke up, then get dressed, catch the bus into town and go to one of the houses where men were going to have sex with me. By the time I turned 13, I had accepted that that was my life and I needed to make the most of it, and after a while I wasn't really afraid of anything. I had drunk enough, often enough, to have gone beyond being numb and beyond the point of pretending, even to myself, that

158

I was having a great time. But as the delusion died, I started to become aggressive, arguing and answering back and telling myself I didn't give a shit about any of it. It got to the point where a clip round the ear from one of the pimps no longer meant anything to me. In fact, violence had become such a constant part of my life that I was no longer really aware of it.

I was playing a potentially dangerous game, however, because I knew what happened to girls who made trouble or didn't do what they were told. For example, one girl I knew had had to have stitches after she was attacked with a glass during an argument. Another, who was one of the girlfriends, tried to leave the guy she was with and when someone put a petrol bomb through her front door, she was quite badly burned and had to jump out of an upstairs window to escape the flames. Fortunately, she survived, and so did her kids, who were in the house with her at the time.

I was lucky though, because I never got really badly beaten up, like some of the other girls did. I think that was partly because of Mum – not because she did anything to keep me safe, but because the fact that they knew I had a mum at home made them more wary about using physical violence to keep me in line. Some of the men had seen me with Sid too, but even the ones who recognised me and smiled at me soon melted away when Sid gave them a look. I suppose they thought he was my grandad, and they weren't going to risk further complicating their already complex lives by messing with him.

Until then, I had always been very careful to watch what I said. Having Asperger syndrome had helped to teach me that it was better to say nothing rather than risk misjudging what was acceptable in a particular situation. But as I began to drink more, I started answering back, arguing with some of the pimps and refusing to go with certain men I didn't like. I only ever did it with pimps like Saleem though, who I was certain wouldn't hit me.

I was 13 when I started going round to Hanif's house. I chose to go there – as much as I 'chose' to do anything – because he gave me vodka and because he didn't like the other guys and didn't have much to do with them. So it was always only him and me. That might have been a good thing, if it hadn't been for the fact that he was an alcoholic and very violent. In the past, I would have hooked up with someone like Hanif because they fed me. But whereas I had only just set out on the road towards alcoholism, he was a good deal further along it and would never have dreamed of spending money on food that could be spent on drink. Despite the way he treated me though, I kept going back. I don't know why. Perhaps it was because it made me feel that I did have some choice. Or perhaps it simply saved me the effort of self-harming.

Hanif would hold me by the throat, pinning me up against a wall, and then have sex with me so violently that my hips would be covered in bruises. I don't think it was violence for its own sake. For me, it was a chance to unleash some of the aggression that was locked away inside me and that I could only release when I was drunk. For Hanif, I think it was all part of a sexual game, particularly when I was drunk and fought back. He could be vicious if I ever actually hurt him though, and on one occasion, after I had given him a bloody nose, he bashed my head on a table so hard I thought I was going to pass out.

One of Hanif's worst tricks was to shut me in the bathroom and lock the door from the outside. There were no windows in his bathroom and the ceiling light was broken. So when the door was closed, it was completely dark in there. I had always been a bit afraid of the dark as a child, and since the Polish guy had tried to rape me, I had become terrified of it. It was the fact that being locked in the bathroom made me panic that was the whole point for Hanif. As soon as he let me out, he would have sex with me, while I was still hysterical and trying to push him away, because having to fight me to get what he wanted turned him on.

It's difficult to explain why I always went back to Hanif's house, despite all the negative aspects of my association with him and however brutal or unkind he was to me. In a strange way, it was almost pleasant to be with someone who was overtly violent. At least everything was out in the open and I knew where I stood, which was preferable, in some ways, to the confusion and bewilderment I always felt when I was the butt of the nasty, undermining comments and the pinches and pushing everyone else subjected me to.

If someone hits you, you get a bruise, which lasts for a few days, then heals and disappears. While the bruise is visible, you can *see* the pain as well as feel it. And at least the person who bruised you was reacting in some way you could understand: you made him angry, so he lashed out at you. It was almost thera-peutic – in a very disturbed way – to witness an unambiguous response to something I had done. What I found much more difficult to deal with was the disinterested indifference of most of the other people who used me. The realisation that I didn't matter at all, even to people like that, made it feel as though every last remnant of 'me' had been sucked out and discarded.

Eight years ago, when this was all happening, there was a lot of coming and going amongst the people I believed I was 'socialising' with. Most of them were asylum seekers who were living in social housing, and therefore often in transit. Migrants from Afghanistan were coming in waves at that time – there would be an influx followed by a quieter period when things settled down politically for a while in their own country. A lot of the asylum seekers would live in a particular town for a while before moving on to bigger cities where they could find employment, or back to their countries of origin if things didn't work out for them here. Some of them stayed though, and after a year or so, the ones who remained began to get tired of me.

As I continued to drink heavily and was no longer a naive little girl, I became less popular, until eventually the texts and phone calls stopped. There were just two guys I was still seeing in the end, and it was while I was in their bedsit one evening that I met Diyan.

Chapter 9

Diyan had sex with me the first time I met him – after his two friends had had their turn. Maybe it was because he was embarrassed and apologetic afterwards that I followed him home later that evening. I kept my distance – like a little stray dog that's desperate for affection but doesn't dare get too close because it's accustomed to being kicked. He knew I was there though and when he eventually turned around and asked 'What are you doing?' I told him simply, 'I have decided to spend the rest of the day with you.' He just looked at me for a few seconds, then shrugged and carried on walking, with me trotting along behind him.

When we arrived at his place, Diyan unlocked the front door and held it open for me. If I *had* been a dog, I would have been wagging my tail as I hurried into the house before he could change his mind. We listened to music while Diyan cooked a meal, then watched telly and ate our dinner sitting side by side on the couch. He didn't try to sleep with me that night, and I left his house in good time to catch the last bus home.

Diyan was 21, and because he knew I was only 13, he kept telling me to go away when I turned up on his doorstep every day, but after about a week he gave in. A 21-year-old having sex with a 13-year-old is abuse by any standards, and I know he was reluctant to get involved with someone so young. But I was determined to make him change his mind, because he was different from all the others. He was gentle and affectionate and treated me the way I had always imagined nice men treated their girlfriends.

I continued to see Hanif for a few weeks, as well as a couple of other guys. Then, as I began to realise that I had found the sort of one-to-one relationship I had always wanted but didn't believe I would ever have, I started spending more and more time with Diyan.

After that first week, I would be waiting outside his house when he got home every day from his work in a supermarket warehouse. He would sigh when he saw me. But he always held the door open with his foot so that I could follow him into the narrow hallway. Then he would cook dinner for us, while I watched cartoons on his TV. That was one of the things I liked about him, the fact that he didn't ever make fun of me for laughing at childish cartoons, like everyone else did.

As our relationship developed, we sometimes went out for dinner or spent a day at the beach. He even introduced me to a couple of his friends, who lived in another town and didn't know my history, so were nice to me and didn't talk *about* me as though I wasn't there. He kept me away from everyone else though, because he liked me, I suppose, and because of my track record.

On the days when Diyan had to work a 12-hour shift, I would get into his flat by climbing through a broken window, then sit on his bed, watching television and drinking cans of cider while I waited for him to come home. Diyan drank quite a bit too – I don't think I knew anyone who didn't – and there was always an eight-pack of cider in his kitchen.

Saleem had a flat in the same house and sometimes, after I'd had a couple of cans, I would get bored of waiting for Diyan to come home from work and go and see Saleem. I slept with him on a couple of occasions and when Diyan found out he was really hurt. But he didn't know what to do about it. He knew that Saleem and the others had exploited me, although he didn't know any of the details of what had been going on. He did try to talk to me about it, and asked me, 'What is it you're not getting from me that makes you want to go back to them? What power have they got over you?' The problem was, neither of us really had the language to discuss it properly and I knew I wouldn't be able to make him understand. I suppose the truth was that I didn't understand it either. So, in the end, he just accepted the fact that there must be some reason why I would go back there other than simply to cheat on him.

After a while, I think my immaturity began to frustrate him, and when he found out I had slept with someone else too, he got really angry with me. 'Just grow up and stop going to them,' he snapped at me. 'Why would you go back there when they've treated you so badly?' That's when it dawned on me that I was going to lose him if I carried on doing what I was doing. So I cut out everyone else, except for one guy called Dev, who was a homeless alcoholic I had met in the park but didn't ever sleep with.

One evening, Dev and I had been drinking together and I was walking back to Diyan's flat when I accidentally bumped into a police officer. It was my fault – I was very drunk and unsteady on my feet – but when he pushed me away, I turned round and spat at him. Before I realised what was happening, he had me in handcuffs and was bundling me into the back of a police car.

When we arrived at the police station and I was told that I would be kept in a cell overnight, I told them, with a stroppy assurance I didn't actually feel, 'You can't do that. You can't keep me here. I'm only 13.' Understandably, in view of the fact that some drunken girl had just gobbed at him, the police officer was unsympathetic and sounded even more hostile than I was when he said, 'Don't try to bullshit me. You're not 13.'

But they did try to phone my mum, and when I refused to give them her number, they brought in a youth advocate to talk to me. They tracked Mum down eventually though, but it was another four or five hours before she came to the police station, during which time I was locked in a cell on my own.

Mum doesn't drive, so she came with her cousin Cora. By the time they arrived, some of the alcohol had worked its way out of my system and I felt bad when I saw how distressed Cora was about what had happened – whereas Mum was so stoned she was barely coherent. I was upset because my glasses had been taken away before I was put in the cell. I suppose they were afraid I might use the lenses to slit my wrists, but the fact that I can hardly see without them made me feel vulnerable and anxious, which did nothing to improve my already belligerent attitude.

In circumstances like that, you would expect most parents to apologise and be very embarrassed by their child's behaviour. Some mothers might even have given me a clip round the ear for doing what I had done. But Mum just thought it was funny. It was almost like having an out-of-body experience, sitting in the police station with Cora, quite literally, wringing her hands with dismay and Mum almost hysterical with laughter. I hate being in situations like that. For someone who sometimes struggles to distinguish between normal and abnormal, Mum's reaction was particularly bewildering and unnerving.

Even after he had met my mum and witnessed her peculiar behaviour, the policeman still clearly blamed me for what had happened – and I can't deny that it *was* my fault for spitting at him. When he discovered that I had been telling the truth and really was only 13, he told Mum, 'She's got a real attitude problem, your kid. She's going to get herself into serious trouble before she's much older.'

What he didn't realise was that it was all an act. The alcohol gave me a confidence I never had when I was sober. I suppose that was one of the things I liked about being drunk: before I got to the point of having drunk so much that I did stupid things like spit at policemen, alcohol enabled me to talk to people and join in conversations with a false assurance I didn't otherwise have. The problem is you don't engage your brain when you're drunk. Any information that comes in through your eyes or ears bypasses it completely and your limbs move automatically, without the benefit of moderating thought.

In the end, the police let me go and Cora drove us back to Mum's house. Even at that age, and with my somewhat tenuous, Asperger-slanted grasp on reality, I remember thinking, 'This is England. Surely someone must be concerned about a drunk 13-year-old girl who has been arrested, whose mother couldn't be contacted for several hours and then turned up at the police station stoned and incoherent.'

Mum had always told me that if I got into trouble with the police, I would be taken into care, and I knew that some of the girls who had taken my place when Saleem stopped being my pimp lived in care homes. They used to talk about them, on the occasions when I had drunk enough alcohol to be able to summon up the courage to join in their conversations. Almost all of them said the homes 'weren't too bad'. One 16-year-old girl lived in a place where staff members were only present in the evenings and for a couple of hours every morning. 'For the rest of the day I can do what I want,' she told me. 'I get money to buy my own clothes and any other things I need. I cook my own food, and I come and go without anyone asking me stupid questions.'

It sounded quite good to me, so I hadn't actually been dreading the fuss I thought would result from my brush with the police. In fact, it was a while before I stopped half-expecting a social worker in an A-line skirt to turn up on our doorstep one day and bundle me away. Perhaps part of me almost wished that it would happen. But, apparently, no one was bothered about the girl who the spat-upon policeman had predicted would 'get herself into serious trouble before she's much older'. Certainly, the knock on the door never came.

Instead, I got a bit of paper and a reprimand for 'assaulting a police officer', which stayed on my record until earlier last year, when I turned 21. I didn't even think at the time how it might be affect things for me in the future. Even if I had had any thoughts of having a career, I couldn't have anticipated the questions that would require careful answers when I subsequently applied for a job. I was just lucky that, six years later, my potential employer was prepared to take into account the fact that it had happened when I was so young.

If I had done the same thing today – spat at a policeman when I was drunk on the streets at the age of 13 – I expect a red flag *would* have been raised. If it had done so then, I can't help wondering what the next few years of my life would have been like.

Diyan was always very paranoid about the police and anxious in case any trouble I got into ended up involving him. 'It's going to come back to my door,' he told me. But he was the only person who was really worried about what had happened at the time – apart from Cora, who never really says very much about anything, but who I knew was shocked and distressed by what I had done.

For the next two or three years, Diyan was pretty much my world. He was the only friend I had and the only person I ever saw. Going from one extreme to another created its own difficulties though, and the fact that our relationship was so intense and we were always under each other's feet began to lead to friction and arguments.

My mental health had started to deteriorate too. Or, at least, the fact that I had problems was becoming more apparent. I didn't have any way of giving vent to the distress that had been building up inside me for months before I met Diyan. Sometimes, when it became too much for me to contain or suppress, it came out in the form of uncontrollable anger. It was as if I was so used to being in flight-or-fight mode that now that I no longer had any need either to flee or fight, the negative energy kept building up inside me until it erupted. I think that, by creating an outlet for my own self-loathing, the sexual exploitation I had been subjected to was almost like a form of self-harming. And now that I was out of that situation, I had terrible rages.

To begin with, Diyan didn't ever retaliate when I lost control and turned on him. He just did his best to protect himself and to restrain me. Although he wasn't very big, maybe 5 foot 8 or 9, he was several inches taller than me. So, fortunately, he was usually able to deflect my attacks, which was lucky, for both of us, because on one occasion I went for him with a knife and if he hadn't managed to prise it out of my hand, I might have done him some real harm. I did cut his face one day though, when I hurled a glass coffee pot at his head.

My attacks on Diyan were almost always a result of paranoia. If he spoke to another girl, for example, I would be immediately convinced that he had had enough of me and was going to leave me. I hadn't ever had anything good before I met him. He was the first person who had wanted to talk to me and to have a normal relationship with me – or as normal as a relationship can be that involves an adult and a 13-year-old child. So I was convinced, and very afraid, that someone was going to snatch him away from me. And because I didn't have the language to express verbally how I felt, it came out in the form of sudden outbursts of temper. Even if I had been able to explain it to him, however, I didn't think Diyan would understand. Why should he? No one had ever understood before – not my teachers or the social workers who had been involved, briefly, when I was at primary school; not even Mum.

I think I felt as though I didn't deserve things to go well for me, certainly not as well as they were going during the first few months of my relationship with Diyan. It's the only rationalisation I can think of that would explain why I pressed the self-destruct button and redirected my life back into the tailspin that was more familiar to me. Eventually, when I did try to halt the process of destruction of the one good thing

I had ever had, everything I did simply made it worse. With my world falling apart, I focused even more single-mindedly on drinking.

I was staying at Diyan's flat three or four nights a week, so I kept some clothes there, and anything else I used on a daily basis. I got up with him every morning, then went back to bed for a couple of hours after he had gone to work. When I got up again and got dressed, I often went to the local library, to return books I had read and to borrow new ones. Then I would go back to the flat, pick up some cans of cider, walk down to a park where I knew I wouldn't bump into any of the guys I used to hang out with, and spend the rest of the day reading and drinking. Although I no longer *started* the day with a can of cider, I would usually drink between two and four cans while I was at the park, then share a bottle of vodka with Diyan in the evening and have another couple of cans of cider plus maybe one or two of Fosters.

I was perfectly happy just reading all day. I had read all the Harry Potter books by that time and was into Victorian family sagas. Sitting on a park bench in a world that didn't seem to have anything good in it for me, I would get completely lost in the world that was created in those books. I know that they weren't great literature. In fact, most of them were variations on the same theme: a poor girl from the slums meets a rich man who sees her for who she really is, falls in love with her, marries her and takes her to live with him in his fabulous mansion. But I really enjoyed them and would read one every three or four days. That was all I had: books to show me a world in which everything turns out well, and alcohol to dull the reality of the world in which it doesn't.

Diyan bought all our food and gave me a fiver every day to buy myself a chocolate bar and a newspaper, or anything else I might fancy. He paid for other things too. For example, if we went shopping and he bought himself some trainers, he would also buy some for me. I hardly saw Mum at all during that period. Although I went home every few days to do my washing and pick up some clean clothes, she was often asleep when I arrived and had already gone out before I got up the next day. She still left a window open for me: I never did have a key to Mum's house. But I had a bed in my room by that time, and if she put her head round my bedroom door in the morning and found me there, asleep, she would leave a cup of tea for me on the sideboard in the living room.

Diyan used to drop me off at the house whenever I went home and one day he came in when Mum was there, so I introduced them. Mum seemed fine about it at the time. But later, after she had met him on a few more occasions, she started going on about him whenever she saw me, saying that he shouldn't be sleeping with someone underage and that she was going to get the police involved. I think that's what people call shutting the stable door after the horse has bolted! She knew I had slept with other men before Diyan, so I didn't understand what her objection was to him specifically. Maybe she just took a dislike to him for some reason, or maybe she was jealous because she could see that we were close, and because I wasn't going home every night like I used to do before I started seeing him.

One evening, when Diyan drove me home and came into the house, Mum and I got into an argument. She was annoyed because she said the only reason I ever went home at all was to use the washing machine. She was right, so her complaint was justified. But what really shocked Diyan was the fact that as she was shouting at me – 'What makes you think you have an automatic right to use *my* washing machine? Why don't you use *his*, seeing as how you're always round there?' – she was also pulling my hair and trying to scratch my face.

I don't think Diyan had ever seen a mother and daughter engage in a physical fight before. He was really worried about me after that and didn't want me to go home at all. For me though, those fights were losing their impact. I had always found them incredibly unnerving and upsetting – even the ones that occurred when I was very young, many of which I probably instigated when something had frightened or frustrated me. But I was already getting to the point when I began to realise that I was physically stronger than my mum and that I didn't need to be scared of her anymore. I had stopped attacking *her* some time before the incident that was witnessed by Diyan, and would only restrain her when she attacked me. It would be a few more years before I reached the conclusion that I should feel sorry for her rather than afraid of her, but the seed of that idea had already planted itself in my mind.

If Mum had been hoping to drive a wedge between me and Diyan so that she would see more of me, the row we had that day had quite the opposite effect. I still went home every three or four days though. If I didn't, Mum would text me saying she was going to contact the police. I don't know whether that was because she was genuinely concerned about me, or because she hated me doing anything that made her feel as though she wasn't, ultimately, the one who was in control.

In the end, I did what I usually did when those sorts of situations arose with Mum and told her what I thought she wanted to hear. The next time she asked me about Diyan, I said, 'Oh, I don't see *him* anymore. I'm seeing this other guy now. He's called … Ahmed.' It was a lie that seemed to please her, and one that I elaborated on over the next few months whenever I saw her by telling her about the things I had done with some entirely fictional guy.

Diyan had lived in England for about four years by the time I met him. Although he had grown up in Iran, he was Afghan and a legal refugee, with all the right documents and papers. Perhaps it was because he had always lived surrounded by mountains and countryside that he loved going backpacking in the Brecon Beacons and Black Mountains in Wales. What he liked more than anything was camping on the side of a mountain in a field with a stream running through it. 'No water has ever tasted so clean,' he used to tell me. 'Drinking it makes me think of home.' In fact, he liked the crystal-clear mountain water so much he once filled up several four-litre water bottles so that we could take some home with us in his little car, and was very disappointed when, just a few days later, it had turned brackish and stale.

We went on several of those camping trips and Diyan took lots of photographs, although almost never of the two of us together. He would take a photo of himself, another of me and another of the scenery. I suppose it was because he knew that, due to my age, his relationship with me could land him in serious trouble if anyone ever found out about it.

I really enjoyed those trips with Diyan. We would camp somewhere remote, where it felt as though there was no one else for miles around, which was ideal for me, as I still found interacting with other people difficult and stressful. The only traumatic part of those holidays was packing up and getting ready to go. I still had a lot of anger inside me, and although Diyan tried not to be drawn into the dramas I created every time, I seemed to be so determined to row with someone about something that, on at least a couple of occasions, I attacked him physically and upset him so much I made him cry.

Diyan was really interested in history, so, wherever we went, we would visit all the local monuments and museums. The only problem was that although Diyan spoke good English, he had trouble reading it. It was frustrating for him to have to ask me to read all the information plaques out loud to him, and eventually he persuaded me to teach him to read for himself. First, I went to the library and got him some kids' books. Then, as his reading skills began to improve, I got him books that were meant for teenagers. And, finally, he was able to read novels that had been written for adults.

One of his favourite books, and the one that he was most proud of being able to read by himself, was *A Thousand Splendid Suns* by Khaled Hosseini. It's a really good story, about the friendship between two girls in Afghanistan and what happens to them when the Taliban take over the country. When Diyan read it, I think I was even more proud of him than he was of himself – to begin with. But it took him weeks to finish it and he insisted on reading every line out loud – slowly, very laboriously and usually while I was trying to watch television. So that, in the end, I almost wished I hadn't taught him to read at all!

Diyan and I were together for almost three years. There were a few hiccups in our relationship, most of them due to my mental health, although I didn't understand what was wrong at the time.

I would sometimes get terrible panic attacks, often in what should have been relatively unthreatening situations, such as being served in a shop. I dreaded shopping. I was convinced that everyone was staring at me because they knew about all the things I had done and because they thought – as I did, on some subconscious level – that I had no right to be there, doing my shopping with all the normal, decent people.

If a shop assistant asked if they could help me, I would feel my face flush with embarrassment and my throat would constrict so that I couldn't swallow and could barely breathe. Then a huge wave of panic would wash over me and Diyan would almost have to push me out of the shop so that he could try to calm me down. I hadn't ever heard of panic attacks, so I thought that whatever it was that happened to me on those occasions *only* happened to me. The whole experience was so humiliating and frightening that I eventually tried to avoid going anywhere there would be other people who might speak to me or require me to speak to them.

Diyan was incredibly patient with me and really did try to help me. But he didn't know what was wrong with me any more than I did.

Chapter 10

At first, I think Diyan believed he could make me better just by loving me. But when he had given me as much love as he possibly could and I was still having apparently random fits of temper and panic attacks, he began to get frustrated with me and would sometimes ask me, irritably, why I didn't 'just deal with it'.

I know he felt uncomfortable about what had happened to me before I met him. He didn't know any specific details; just that some of men who had abused me were Afghan, like he was. I think that created a dilemma in his mind, because although what they had done to me was unequivocally wrong, it would have felt like criticising men who were his friends if he had taken my side against them. I can understand how he felt. The thought that someone you've grown up with would rape and abuse a child is a thought no one would want to examine too closely, particularly if they didn't know how they would deal with any of the issues it might give rise to.

Whenever I went away with Diyan – to the seaside or camping in Wales – I told Mum I had been with Ahmed. I knew how her mind worked by that time, so I played it to my advantage. And just to make sure she got the message that Diyan wasn't of any consequence to me, I sometimes mentioned other names too and said things like, 'Did I tell you I've been seeing Mohammed?' or 'When I was out with Lamar the other night …'. Strange as it may sound, Mum seemed to be more comfortable with the idea that I was seeing lots of different men than she had been with the thought that I was seeing just one.

I had been with Diyan for almost two years, so was 14 when he did something for me that was probably the single most important thing anyone has ever done for me before or since. He persuaded me to go back to school. His maths was brilliant, and while I was teaching him to read and write in English, he was teaching me to understand the numerals that had always been as indecipherable to me as the hieroglyphics of some ancient language.

We did a lot of work together. But because I had struggled to cope with the confusion of the classroom and had ultimately stopped going to school at a young age, I had never really done any writing. And when Diyan asked me questions I couldn't answer, he would tell me, 'This is basic English. You are English. You should be able to do this with your eyes shut. You have *got* to get some education.' It seemed that someone at social services thought so too. Because, one day, Mum sent me a text telling me to come home as a meeting had been arranged for the following morning.

After I had 'opted out' of secondary school, I had been given a laptop for home schooling, which I hadn't logged on to for the last four or five months. In fact, it had got me into trouble at one point, when someone checked it and discovered that I had looked up several 'inappropriate websites'. It was actually during the time when I had been trying to understand what was happening to me and had researched 'sex' and 'rape'. What was *really* 'inappropriate', however, when I think about it now, is the fact that my inappropriate internet history didn't raise any red flags and no one thought to question *why* a 12-year-old child had been looking at the sort of websites I had been looking at.

I went home when I got the text from Mum, although I had no intention at that time of getting involved in whatever sort of schooling social services might have in mind for me.

'We've got this brand new idea,' the social worker told me when she came to the house the next day. 'It's called a pupil referral unit. It's one-to-one teaching, so it's ideal for someone like you.' I wasn't sure what aspect of someone like me she thought it would be ideal for, but she was so upbeat and enthusiastic about it all that I couldn't help feeling a bit mean when I shrugged my shoulders and said 'Nah.'

Later that day, when I went back to Diyan's flat and told him what the social worker had said, he was almost as excited about it as she was. 'It's brilliant,' he told me. 'You can't cope with other people, so surely one-to-one teaching is exactly what you need? Why don't you give it a go?'

I gave him the same monosyllabic answer I had given the social worker. But Diyan wasn't as easily dissuaded as she had been. 'You've *got* to,' he insisted. 'Come on, Taylor. The only reason you haven't got any education is because you couldn't cope with all the other kids and the noise in the classroom. It isn't because you aren't able to learn. You're not stupid. But you might as well be if you can't ever get a decent job because you haven't been to school.'

Fortunately for me, Diyan was easily the most mature and persistent person I had ever known. And, eventually, I agreed, if only to shut him up.

In fact, the social worker had been quite nice and her enthusiasm turned out to be genuine. She was just out of university, in her early twenties, and still idealistic enough to want to engage with young people like me on our own wavelength. Even though I had turned down her suggestion with enough conviction to have persuaded her that I really wasn't interested in attending the pupil referral unit, she had given me her phone number. A couple of days later, I sent her a text telling her I had changed my mind and had decided to give it a go.

After I had enrolled, I began to spend more time at home, because that was where the taxi picked me up in the mornings on the three days a week that I attended classes. I have lots of reasons to be grateful to Diyan. Perhaps the most important one of all is because he was the person who pushed me into going back to school. I really loved it there – so much so, in fact, that I ended up staying for two years, which enabled me to go on to college and gave me an opportunity to do something with my life that, otherwise, I would almost certainly never have had.

In the second year, when I went up to the next class, I started working with some of the other students. But, for the first year, it was just me and my teachers. Although I had been able to read for as long as I could remember, when I started at the unit I was barely able to write a coherent sentence or add 2 + 2, despite Diyan's best attempts to teach me some maths.

My main teacher, Dawn, helped me with English and maths, and also got me interested in poetry. Another teacher, Cathy, did art and fashion design. They were both really nice. What was even more important, however, was that they didn't think I was weird or stupid for not knowing even the basics.

As the pupil referral unit had a very low budget, the teachers' petrol allowance didn't stretch to driving pupils to visit museums and art galleries. So Cathy and I would scour all the charity shops for clothes and shoes that I would then adapt and redesign to create my own 'works of art'.

It wasn't like being at school at all. I didn't get confused or frustrated and no one ever laughed at me because I didn't understand something. Later, when a building was allocated to the pupil referral unit, we had our classes there. Until then, we worked in the local library or a coffee shop, or in the park if it was a nice day.

When we did move into the building, I added cookery to my developing skills. In fact, it became one of my favourite classes. I've got this weird thing about trying to do anything new. I still struggle with it today. I suppose it comes from so often feeling humiliated and embarrassed. If I am forced to do something I don't really know *how* to do, I become almost hysterical. That's why I hated it when Diyan tried to teach me to cook. It wasn't that I *couldn't* do it; I just couldn't cope with the thought that I was going to make a mistake. But Dawn and Cathy were so patient with me and so completely non-judgemental that when I did things with them, I didn't mind if I got something wrong. It took me a while to accept the fact that nobody was going to laugh at me or call me an idiot if I burned the potatoes. Then I stopped being anxious and started to enjoy myself – and ended up being able to cook a pretty good three-course meal!

Later, in the second year, when the pupil–teacher ratio changed from 1:1 to 3:1, I did construction too. I worked on a farm with some of the other kids, demolishing an old pre-fab building with sledge hammers and learning brick-laying skills so that we could build new walls. None of the teachers had ever taught in conventional schools and the guy who did construction with us swore like a trooper, but was really good at managing kids who objected to following rules.

It was a brilliant way of giving disaffected young people, like me, the chance to learn without feeling pressured and inadequate. I don't know if pupil referral units still exist today and, if they do, if they're anything like the one I went to. It would be a shame if the teachers are no longer allowed to adapt their methods to suit the needs of individual kids. But I suspect I was just lucky to be involved at the outset, when they *were* able to be flexible and to make their own decisions about the best way to encourage and engage kids who had been alienated from education – for whatever reason – in more traditional school environments.

As funny as it might sound, I think the reason why they chose me to be one of their guinea-pig pupils was because I was a 'good' disengaged child. Apart from a couple of occasions when I kicked off with teachers at primary school, I didn't have any history of violence or any record of juvenile convictions, which meant that it didn't require three professionals to risk assess me. I was just a kid who hadn't been attending school. So I was an ideal candidate for testing the project – which turned out to be very lucky for me. For the first time in my life, I was learning something useful while doing something I really enjoyed and I actually looked forward to those three days a week.

Things at home weren't going so well, however. I suppose it's a case of be careful what you wish for. Because although Mum hadn't liked the fact that I was spending so much time with Diyan – or with Ahmed, Lamar and all the other imaginary characters she believed I was seeing – she didn't really like it any better when I was at home. It didn't take long for us to adopt the roles of polite, barely connected strangers who spoke to each other only in the interrogative – 'Had a good day?', 'Yes, thanks, and you?', 'Yes, good, thanks. Want a cup of tea?' It was all manageable though. What helped was that by that time I had stopped wishing I had a good relationship with my mum and was just happy that we no longer got involved in physical fights.

But they say that the past casts a long shadow. And mine was about to catch up with me.

Part of the plan to get me back on the radar and into education involved sending a taxi to my house to pick me up on school mornings and another to take me home from town at the end of the day. It wasn't a large town, so I suppose it shouldn't have been as shocking as it seemed to me at the time to discover that the taxi company used by the pupil referral unit employed some of the men who used to have sex with me at parties.

The first time it happened, I was already seat-belted into the front passenger seat and the taxi was pulling out into the traffic by the time I recognised the driver. I turned away quickly, hoping he hadn't seen the expression of horrified dismay I hadn't been quick enough to conceal. But although neither of us said anything, I was certain he had recognised me too. It turned out that I was right. When he reached across and put his hand on my knee, it felt as though an electric shock had passed through my body. Fortunately, when I jerked my leg away from him and said 'No' a bit more loudly and emphatically than I had intended, he just made a dismissive, contemptuous sound and didn't try to touch or speak to me again.

What was even more distressing than having had to sit in a car beside one of my abusers, however, was the thought that he now knew where I lived. I don't know what I imagined he might do with that knowl-edge – realistically, he wasn't going to come knocking on the door demanding that I had sex with him. But for the next 30 minutes, until he dropped me off outside the café where I was meeting Dawn, all the positive things that were happening in my life suddenly seemed trivial compared with the realisation that I might never be able to escape from my past.

Given the choice, I would never have sat in the front seat of a taxi again. But our house was on a narrow country lane and when the drivers pulled over to pick me up, close to a bend in the road, I had to jump in quickly, and sometimes the back door was locked. Now, I would ask a driver to open it. But I didn't have the confidence to speak out then. So I would sit in the front, hoping the taxi driver would be a man I didn't know, or one who had had sex with me without looking at my face.

It was a 40-minute journey from our house to the pupil referral unit when it moved into a building in town. So I did eventually start insisting on sitting in the back of the taxis that came to pick me up. But even then I would keep my head bowed and my eyes fixed on my phone as I counted the minutes until we arrived.

There were a couple of taxi drivers – men who had been quite violent with me at the parties – who I wouldn't have got into a car with under any circumstances. I had come across one of them for the first time when I was 12. We were hanging around outside one of the kebab shops in town and he had let me sit in his car with him, listening to music. It was a hot day in the summer and we were sitting with the car doors open. So when he told me to 'Close the door' I assumed he just wanted to turn on the air conditioning and did it without even thinking.

When I heard the locks click, I felt a prickling sensation on the back of my neck, which quickly developed into full-blown panic when he started the engine and roared off down the road. I kept pleading with him to stop and let me out of the car, but he just laughed. In fact, my obvious fear seemed to spur him on to take more risks as he sped through the streets like a maniac.

I always knew I was pretty safe as long as Saleem or one of the other pimps was around: it was unlikely that anyone would dare to beat me up knowing that they would then have to face whoever 'owned' me. There was no one to protect me in this guy's car though, and I didn't know where he was taking me or what he was going to do. Fortunately, he just wanted to frighten me. But when he turned up at the house in his taxi one morning to take me to school, there was no way I was going to get into it. So I told him I had changed my mind and sent him away.

I did that on other days too, with other taxi drivers, for similar reasons. I hated doing it, because I wanted to go to the unit and learn, and because I couldn't ever tell anyone *why* I hadn't gone in, so I felt as though I was letting my teachers down. Some of the taxi drivers were okay. But the fact that some of them were linked to my past often made the journey to and from the unit very stressful, which took all the pleasure out of going somewhere I really wanted to go. Fortunately though, the taxi drivers must have worked on a rota system and the worst ones only turned up a couple of times a month. So I continued to go to school on most days for the next couple of years.

Otherwise, things *were* going well. Mum was doing her own thing and leaving me to do mine, and it felt as though Diyan and I were moving towards the future, if not hand in hand, then certainly side by side. If he hadn't encouraged me to go to school, I doubt whether I would ever have discovered poetry or been able to write anything more complicated than a shopping list. There was one problem, however, which was that he was quite unhappy in this country.

Diyan was sending a substantial amount of all the money he earned back to his family in Iran. And as the months passed and the pressure on him began to increase, he lashed out at me a few times. Sometimes he hit me across the face with the back of his hand or strangled me, and on one occasion he pushed me down the stairs. He only ever did it when he was drunk and he always cried and apologised afterwards. But although it might sound like the sort of excuse a victim of domestic violence would make, it really wasn't ever malicious. Diyan wasn't a violent person by nature and I know he didn't actually want to hurt me. It was just that we were both trapped in an intense situation. We didn't have other friends or anything else in our lives. All we had was each other, and for our own, individual reasons, we were finding our life together increasingly difficult to cope with.

By the time we had been together for a couple of years, I had begun to find Diyan quite controlling. I was 15 and as I began to grow up, I wanted to spend more time on my own. But whenever I tried to go out without him, he would ask, 'Where are you going? Who are you seeing? Are you all right? What are you up to?' I knew he was just concerned for my well-being and that it was perfectly reasonable for him to ask those questions of someone with my past. And in some ways he was right to be apprehensive, because I *was* seeing someone else, although not in any way that would have threatened my relationship with Diyan.

When I was attending the pupil referral unit and had begun to widen my previously very narrow horizons, both intellectually and in terms of meeting people, I found it a bit restricting spending all the rest of my time with Diyan. Sometimes, I felt as though I was being suffocated by his anxiety about keeping me safe. Maybe it was that feeling that caused me to start drinking more heavily again. Or maybe it was the realisation that now that I was beginning to live the sort of life I always thought I wanted to live, it didn't seem to be as great or as uncomplicated as I had hoped and expected it to be.

I still enjoyed going to the pupil referral unit, but I was beginning to feel as though I wasn't really *doing* anything. I suppose it's the way most teenagers feel at some stage – bored and frustrated because they suddenly find themselves in an apparent no-man's land between childhood and adulthood, but aren't yet able to start leading their own lives.

I felt trapped by my own very small experience. I didn't know that any mainstream options would be open to me. After having missed so much of my education before the age of 14, I didn't dream that I might be able to go to college, for example. I had very low self-confidence, as well as mental-health issues that made the prospect of going anywhere seem even more daunting than the prospect of having to stay where I was. It was the sort of frustration that could make even a fairly even-tempered 15-year-old feel restless and angry. And I wasn't particularly even-tempered at the best of times.

When my relationship with Diyan started to feel repressive and stultifying, I began to spend more time with Dev, the alcoholic guy in his late thirties who I had met a couple of years earlier at the park and who lived in a filthy, rat-infested squat. I loved Dev to bits and really enjoyed his company. He made me feel safe too, because although in the normal course of events he wouldn't have been able to fight his way out of a wet paper bag, he went absolutely nuts if anyone attempted to lay a finger on me. Perhaps one of the main bonds that existed between us, though, was our shared dependence on alcohol.

Diyan simply didn't know what to do about it all. He expected better of me and I felt ashamed because I was letting him down. I was already angry with the world in general, and when I began to feel guilty about the way I was treating Diyan, I felt angry with him too, and that made me cynical. Although I still loved him, I started to find his sweetness and naivety annoying. I decided it was stupid of him to believe that his love, all the little gifts he bought for me and all the nice things he did for me, could make my problems go away.

I kept my friendship with Dev hidden from him, because I thought if Diyan knew about him he might confront him and I didn't want to see either of them get hurt in a fight. But he knew I was seeing *someone* at the park, someone who was encouraging me to drink and whose influence he didn't approve of. That was why he always made sure there were some cans of cider in the house while he was at work, so that I didn't *have* to go out to buy alcohol and to see whoever it was he knew I was seeing.

It breaks my heart now when I think about how much effort Diyan put into trying to help me, and how it only made me even angrier. It was the same problem I always suffered from – in my mind, I didn't deserve his love or what he was trying to do for me. Without consciously realising it, I think I wanted him to hate me as much as I hated myself. When he continued to love me despite my bad behaviour, I told myself it was because he was stupid and was refusing to see things the way they really were. Because I was so certain that I was right and he was wrong, I created arguments out of nothing, until, slowly but surely, I sabotaged my relationship with the one person who really did want what was best for me.

As well as encouraging me to go back to school, it was Diyan who had supported me – financially and in any other way he could – while I was there and who actually enjoyed spending time with me. But instead of showing any gratitude for everything he had done and was continuing to do for me, I spent more and more time with Dev, strutting openly around town with him and picking fights with random girls, until eventually Diyan's friends began to ask him, 'Did you know your girlfriend was seeing some old alcoholic?' Quite apart from the effect my blatant disloyalty must have had on Diyan, I was risking ending up in trouble with the police again and maybe this time getting put in juvenile detention.

Chapter 11

If Diyan couldn't give me a lift to somewhere I wanted to go, he used to give me money for the bus. One evening, I had popped home to Mum's to get a change of clothes and was sitting on a bus heading back into town when I took a dislike to some girl and started staring at her. I thought I was so hard. But really I was being incredibly stupid. When I got off the bus, I decided to have the 'last word' and slammed my fist into the window right beside where the girl was sitting. Although it gave her a very satisfying fright, the glass didn't break, of course. But one of my knuckles did.

I have always been wary of going to the doctor, so when I got to Diyan's flat, he bandaged my hand for me, then rooted around in his first-aid box and found me something to take for the pain. In fact, Diyan was a bit of a hypochondriac, so his first-aid box was the size of a suitcase and contained what, for anyone else, would have been more than a lifetime's supply of bandages, tablets, ointments and any other odds and ends that he might ever conceivably need.

I used to laugh at him about it, but it was actually quite fortunate for me, because I was accident prone, particularly during the periods when I was drinking heavily. I have broken toes – on two separate occasions – by kicking walls when I was in a bad mood. I have fallen down stairs and broken my wrist, which Diyan also bandaged up for me but which never set properly and is still misshapen and sometimes painful. And one night, when I was very drunk and making a cup of tea in Diyan's little kitchenette, I dropped the kettle and spilled boiling water all over my feet.

He never said anything when I came home damaged and dejected. He simply examined my latest injury, dug around in his first-aid box, administered whatever pills and potions were required, and then put me to bed to sleep it off. Remarkably, the boiling water didn't leave any scars on my feet, and I came through most of the other incidents relatively unscathed too – certainly a good deal better than I would have done without Diyan's help. In fact, I don't know whether I would have survived those three years without him.

During the last couple of years I was with Diyan, I was spending time with Saleem too. Because his flat was in the same house and they both worked at the same place, Diyan often gave him a lift in the mornings. But they didn't actually like each other and didn't ever socialise together. When they were working different shifts, I used to hang out in Saleem's room sometimes, getting stoned, while Diyan was still at work. I wasn't sleeping with Saleem. I was past my sell-by-date as far as he was concerned and he had other girls he was pimping for by that time, 'new' girls between the ages of 14 and 17, who were more easily cajoled and coerced.

Saleem still held parties, although they were much smaller events than they had been when I was involved, usually with just two or three guys and two or three girls and only the occasional threesome. To me, that was further proof of something I already suspected – that it was my fault the parties I went to turned out the way they did for me. I thought that the reason I had been so badly abused must have been because of something I was doing wrong, particularly in view of the fact that the parties had been presented to me as such a fun idea.

There was a large lounge upstairs in the house, where the girls used to hang out, and I started going up there too, hoping that I would get the chance to join in and have a drink with them. But I had never had any friends of my own age and I didn't know how to act or what to say to the other girls. I used to stand there for half an hour, watching silently from the sidelines, feeling embarrassed and uncomfortable, then edge my way out of the door again, as inconspicuously as possible, and go back down to Diyan's flat.

When I started projecting some of the anger I felt towards myself on to other people – like the perfectly innocent girl in the bus – I would sometimes pick fights with the other girls. One day, when there was a party in the house and some girl started mouthing off at me, calling me stupid and ugly, I pushed her down the stairs. I was drunk, which always made me even less able than usual to express myself verbally, and just gave her a shove, without having any real intention of hurting her. Fortunately, she was drunk too, and she wasn't badly hurt. It wasn't until much later that I realised how easily it could have ended in disaster – for both of us. But it was after that incident that I started avoiding everyone, although I did continue to smoke weed with Saleem.

My mental health was already precarious and the cannabis only made it worse, until eventually I was so paranoid I became convinced that everyone was laughing at me. The more paranoid I became, the more time I spent drinking with Dev and strutting around town looking for reasons to air my attitude problem. And when I wasn't doing that, I was sitting alone in Diyan's room, listening to music with a can of cider in my hand.

It was being alone that I found really difficult – just like my mum, I suppose. I hadn't ever been on my own before. My earliest memories are of being surrounded by people when Mum and I lived in Cora's flat, which became the doss-house. Then we moved in with Dan and his children. Then, for me, the parties and years of abuse began. Now, though, because of my paranoia, I didn't want the company of other people and I began to isolate myself. I hated myself and everyone else. Eventually, I was so full of anger that I began to hate Diyan too. I treated him very badly at that time. But I didn't really want to be without him. So I was shocked and upset when he told me one day that his British passport had come through and he was going to Iran for a few weeks to visit his family. When he left, I went back to live at Mum's.

Diyan had been away for a couple of weeks when he phoned and told me, casually, 'My family have found me a wife. I'm going to get married.' He said it in the sort of voice you would use if you were telling someone an inconsequential bit of news you thought might be of passing interest to them. But I felt as though all the breath had been punched out of me. It took a huge effort of will to contain the sound, which was somewhere between a scream and a wail of pain, that exploded out of me as soon as I had hung up the phone. I had a bed in my room at Mum's house by that time, and I had been lying on it while I listened to Diyan. Now, I buried my head in my pillow and sobbed.

Mum must have heard me, because she shouted, 'Are you calling me? Taylor? What do you want?'

'Nothing,' I managed to shout back. 'I'm fine. It's okay.' Although the truth was I didn't think I would ever be okay again.

Diyan and I had been together for three years and, despite the way I had been treating him for the last few months, I really did believe that we were going to be together for the rest of our lives. The idea that our relationship was already dead and waiting to be buried was too immense and incomprehensible for me to process. It was so inconceivable, in fact, that I put it to the back of my mind after a couple of days and began to look forward to the day when Diyan was due to come home.

At around the same time as he had left England to go to Iran, I had started college. The pupil referral unit sent me on an introductory course, which included classes in independent living skills, maths, English and ICT. My reasons for wanting to go to college weren't academic, however. I went because I wanted to learn how to socialise and to be with other people, so that I could get on in the world beyond Diyan's bedsit. Which was fortunate, in a way, because it meant that when the course itself turned out to be incredibly boring, I was determined to stick it out.

My mental health was still erratic at that time, but I had good days and was getting to the point of almost being able to control it – at least enough to hold things together when I needed to. I was 16 and restless and I hoped that completing my course at college might enable me to get a proper job and do something interesting with my life. More than that though, I wanted to learn to be normal, and I realised that I could only do that by observing kids of my own age. I was still very self-conscious and convinced that everyone was making fun of me. But I persevered, and eventually I did make some connections, although not the sort of friendships that would have involved meeting up with people in evenings and at weekends.

It took me years to learn how to act normally and to master the skills that enable me today to deal with simple, everyday interactions. If someone patted me on the shoulder, for example, I would react by jumping out of my skin or spinning round and slapping them, because I thought they were going to shove or hit me. It was mortifying to react like that to every sound anyone made behind me, and it was a huge relief when I was learned to conceal my panic and not respond visibly in any way. I did so well, in fact, that I even learned the art of telling a joke!

Diyan was supposed to be away for two months, but he ended up staying in Iran for almost three. I kept telling myself, 'I love him enough to be able to ignore the fact that he's got a wife. She's in another country. She's not going to affect me.' When he finally came back, however, his new wife was all he wanted to talk about. He showed me photographs of their wedding and of all the places they had visited together and didn't seem to be able to understand why I wasn't happy for him. I suppose the way I had been behaving before he left had made him believe that, certainly from my perspective, our relationship had run its course. So I couldn't blame him for taking the opportunity that had been offered to him to move on.

The truth was, I was devastated. Although Diyan hadn't ever said anything specifically to make me believe it would be the case, I had always assumed that when I was 16 we would be able to live openly together, because our relationship would be legitimate and there would no longer be any risk of him getting into trouble because of it. Perhaps it was an assumption I had made simply on the basis of what Tom used to tell me when I was 11.

Diyan had been keeping me for the last three years, but when I was 16 I had planned to get a job, probably in a café, and start paying my share of our living expenses. I had it all worked out in my head: with my income, we would be able to afford to move out of Diyan's bedsit and rent our own flat. We would put money aside every month for holidays, stay in hotels and do all the other things real couples do. I even imagined the children we were going to have, and how we would furnish and decorate the little house we would eventually buy.

I turned 16 while Diyan was in Iran. But when he came back, instead of talking about the future we were going to have together, he showed me a photograph and said, 'This is the woman I have married. I thought you would be happy for me.' That's when I realised that the life I believed we were going to share had never existed except in my own imagination.

Diyan and I often used to walk along the towpath beside the river. It was peaceful and pretty, and I had really enjoyed those walks to begin with. Then, before he went to Iran, I started to get bored of doing the same old things. He was happy doing normal couply things, like cooking a meal, watching television and just being at home in the evenings. He liked routine. It made him feel secure to go to the supermarket every Saturday or stroll along the same stretch of beach we had visited a hundred times before. But I wasn't interested anymore in sitting with him on the swings at the children's play park, watching the sun set in a glow of colour across the river. Perhaps I had grown so complacent in my belief that we would always be a couple, I felt safe wanting to go to parties and do all the other things 16-year-olds want to do rather than what I saw as mundane 'couple things'.

I sometimes got frustrated with Diyan and told myself he was stupid. But it was only because I was angry with the world and sceptical of his belief that love and kindness could make bad things better. The truth was that I loved him. He had been my whole world for almost three years and the only good thing I had ever had for as long as I could remember. So although I sometimes lashed out at him, it hadn't ever crossed my mind that, when he came back from Iran, we wouldn't find the middle ground and be together forever.

The first time I went to see Diyan after he returned from Iran, I slept with him. But I knew that day that everything had changed – for both of us. He was married and planning to bring his wife to England as soon as she got a visa, and I had grown up and moved away from him. We were two totally different people – different from the way we had been three years previously as well as different from each other – and we didn't really understand each other anymore. It was incredibly sad. After we had been together for so long, it was hard enough to admit, even to ourselves, that it was over and neither of us wanted to say it out loud. During the next few days, we gradually drifted further and further apart, and then stopped seeing each other altogether.

* * *

Despite the heartbreak of our separation, I hadn't actually been faithful to, or honest with, Diyan while he was in Iran. There had been a funfair in the local park about a week before he came back and when I went to it one evening, I bumped into a guy called Baashir who worked in a takeaway food place in town. I had chatted to him before, and when I went back to his flat with him that night, we both got paralytically drunk. Even though it was after Diyan had told me on the phone about his marriage, in my mind we were still technically together, so sleeping with Baashir was like cheating on him. Maybe that's why it felt almost like a punishment and why I hated every minute of it and kept thinking, 'I don't want this. I want Diyan.'

Baashir was the first person other than Diyan I had had sex with for more than two years. We didn't use protection that night and I was very worried afterwards in case I had caught an STD or got pregnant. I had grown up a lot since the days when I used to lie on a bed in someone else's house waiting for the door to open and the next faceless man to walk into the room and have sex with me. Being 16 years old and aware of the risks of having sex without contraception might not sound like a very significant marker of responsibility, but it was a real turning point for me.

After that first night, Baashir started following me around town, offering me bags of chips and drinks, and eventually I went with him again because there *was* no one else. I had no feelings for him at all. It was just that being with him seemed like a better option than being on my own, and I needed *someone's* company at that time, because I had recently stopped drinking during the day.

I really wanted to control my mental health and it had become clear, even to me, what effect alcohol was having on it. If I didn't have a drink in the morning, I would get the shakes and feel physically sick. I was getting fed up with not being able to cope. So I began to wean myself off drinking by telling myself, 'Get through the morning and then you can have a drink.' Then, when I had achieved that first self-imposed goal, 'Now just get through the afternoon and you can have a drink tonight.'

Baashir was 19. He had arrived in England as an illegal immigrant from Afghanistan about six months before I met him and had been given a temporary visa. He was actually Pashtun, which is an ethnic group of Muslims who have their own specific religious and ethical traditions. None of the other Pashtun boys I knew had relationships with English girls. But when I became Baashir's girlfriend, he was very protective of me and I knew no one else would dare lay a finger on me. In fact, most of his mates simply ignored me, and I quickly learned to ignore them too.

I didn't love Baashir. What appealed to me about him was the fact that he was everything Diyan wasn't. He liked parties, drinking vodka and doing all the other things I thought young people were supposed to do. After the pain of my break-up with Diyan, he seemed to offer me the perfect opportunity to take life less seriously and lose myself for a while.

I was still clinging to the dream of having a home and a family. Now though, having lost Diyan, I had decided that it didn't really matter *who* made that dream a reality. Baashir had a flat overlooking the river and one evening, when we were watching the sunset from his window and he was standing behind me with his arms around my waist, I suddenly thought, 'Yeah, this will do. I can make it work with Baashir.' I think it was at that moment I realised that, for me, what was really important was the dream itself. If I couldn't make it become reality with Diyan, Baashir would do instead.

In fact, I had become so fixated on chasing my dream of having a home and a family as soon as possible that I allowed it to obscure what should have been the bigger picture. And, as a result, I made a decision that is perhaps my greatest regret.

It was while I was seeing Baashir that I met an English boy called Adam – a normal, 18-year-old teenager who liked to go bowling and whose idea of a meal out was a burger and fries at McDonald's. Adam and I became good friends who enjoyed each other's company and had great times together, laughing and joking around, like normal teenagers do. That in itself was a huge landmark for me, because I had begun to believe that I would never have any 'normal' friendships with people of my own age.

I know Adam thought I was his girlfriend. But when it came to deciding who I really wanted to be with – Adam or Baashir – I chose the dream instead of the more sensible option of waiting, getting a good education, then a job, and going through all the other stages that would have prepared me much better for becoming a wife and mother.

I actually sat down one day and weighed up all the pros and cons on each side. 'Okay, so Adam … I'm happier with Adam. He makes me smile. I feel safe with him. I think I could quite easily fall in love with him. Then there's Baashir … I don't love Baashir. I don't even really care very much about him. But he has got a job. So he would be a better provider and therefore a better father.' When I looked at it like that, in simplistic, black-and-white terms – and bearing in mind my fixation on having my own home and family – the choice seemed obvious.

It was the wrong choice, of course. And although choosing Adam might not have turned out any better, for either of us, I wish I had given it a try. At least then I would have had a few years to be young and the chance to rebuild the childhood I had lost, to stay on at college and get some qualifications that would have given me real choices in life. So yes, when I think about it now, not giving my relationship with Adam a chance is *definitely* my greatest regret.

One of the many mistakes I was making was trying to run when I could barely walk. Losing Diyan felt like losing my security. Perhaps it isn't surprising that, after my experiences during the first 16 years of my life, security was the one thing that really mattered to me – security and the longing for everything just to be *normal*.

I think it was when I was struggling to understand and copy the behaviour of my fellow students that I began to realise, that despite my relatively easy relationship with Adam, I was never going to have a normal life like his, even if, by some miracle, he did become the person I shared my future with.

For a brief period, I had options and opportunities to make a good life for myself. The problem was I didn't have the self-confidence to make the right choice. Instead, I decided that I wasn't cut out for qualifications and that it would be better to stay in my small world. So I dropped out of college and chose Baashir. I still sometimes wonder what might have happened if I had taken a different turning at that particular crossroads in my life.

Since splitting up with Diyan, I had been living back at Mum's. When Baashir moved to a town just a train ride away, I stopped going regularly to college and started spending more time with him. Then, three months after we met at the funfair, we got engaged. Mum didn't approve – whether of Baashir himself, the fact of our engagement, or because I was just 16 was never really clear. Whatever her reasons, she said she had 'tried for years' and that she was now 'washing her hands' of me.

After we got engaged, I more or less moved into Baashir's shared house, where there always seemed to be a party going on. This time, though, I was a guest at the parties and didn't have to sleep with anyone except Baashir. It felt as though I was being given the chance to start again and to rewrite my own history.

Baashir and I often sat together in his bed while he described the little shop he was going to get and the flat above it where we would live and raise our family. After the countless hours I had spent imagining the life I would have with Diyan, it was nice to be able to share someone else's dream and to know that I was a vital part of it.

One of the best things about dreams is that they aren't constrained by reality. In a dream, you can live with a man you love and your perfect children in a beautifully furnished flat above your own, thriving business without having to consider any of the practicalities of the real world. It was that sort of dream we were pursuing when we started trying for a baby.

Chapter 12

Although Baashir was Afghan, he had lived in refugee camps in Pakistan from the age of eight until he came to England at 17. To anyone born and raised in a house with brick walls, decent furniture, heating, hot water and all the other things most of us take for granted, it's impossible to imagine what his childhood must have been like. Whatever else had been missing from mine, at least I had lived, for most of it, in a solid, clean house.

Baashir had a strong personality, which was fascinating to me because I had almost no perceptible personality at all when I was 16, and absolutely no idea who I was. I don't know if it was because of his experiences as a child that he often got involved in physical fights. It was one of the reasons why I was always a bit wary of him, although he didn't ever threaten or frighten me – at least, not to begin with.

There was a lot of anger bottled up inside Baashir, which I could understand, having felt the same way myself for much of the previous five years. Inevitably, his anger would often erupt when he was drunk and he would sometimes walk down a road kicking lamp posts and cars. He attacked his friends, too, when they tried to restrain him so that he didn't damage other people's property or hurt himself. The guys who had been in refugee camps had a bond that united them and set them apart from everyone else. So Baashir's friends never held it against him however many times he lashed out at them and kicked or punched them. Even when he broke someone's nose on one occasion, they all still stuck by him and continued to try to protect him from himself.

Whenever he lost his temper, he didn't ever mention his violence the next day, when he had sobered up. His way of apologising was to slap his friends on the back and ask, 'You all right, mate?' and they would turn and smile at him and tell him they were fine. They had shared the same childhood experiences so they must have felt the same sense of anger and fear themselves; they were just better at hiding it, or perhaps they gave vent to it in different ways. What also helped to retain those friendships was the fact that Baashir was a charmer: when he wasn't drunk or stoned, he was good company and everyone's best friend.

In the first couple of months after we got engaged, I had at least one very early miscarriage. It sounds a terrible thing to say, but I was almost pleased when it happened. I knew I wasn't ready to have a baby. But a child was such an essential part of the dream that, in my mind, becoming a parent came as an indivisible package that included the marriage, the home, the family and the security. I'm ashamed to say that I got pregnant because I was bored too. Becoming a mother and a wife can seem like a good ambition to have when you're 16 years old and don't have any discernible place in society, or anything constructive to do to occupy your time. So we kept trying, and three months after Baashir and I got engaged, I fell pregnant again. And this time it stuck.

I knew I was pregnant even before I took the test. Baashir lived in a shared house, when he wasn't sofa-surfing. I still took my washing home to Mum's, sometimes staying there for two or three days, just to clear my head a bit and get some space. But Baashir was with me when I did the test, crouching behind a bush to pee on the little stick when we went for a walk in the woods.

I knew what the result was going to be even before I looked to see if the indicator had changed colour. But until I had proof I could at least tell myself that there was a chance I was wrong. Baashir was delighted though, when the test turned out to be positive, whereas all I remember thinking was, 'Fuck. That's it now. I'm just going to have to manage.'

I must only have been about three weeks' pregnant when I took the test. I was already working part-time in a café and a few days later I dropped out of college completely. In fact, I got the sack from the café not long afterwards, for telling the owner what I thought about his two sons standing around chatting while I did all their work as well as my own. Maybe someone who wasn't on the autistic spectrum would have made the point more diplomatically! But I was glad, in a way, to lose that job. Although Baashir and I were saving all the money I was earning so that we could get married, the work there was incredibly stressful and I suspect that lugging heavy trays of plates and cutlery around the kitchen might have contributed to my previous miscarriage.

After the café, I started doing work experience in a shopping mall. Retail probably wouldn't be the occupation of choice for anyone who finds social interaction difficult and I found the whole experience quite traumatising. But I had to do something because Baashir's visa had run out so he couldn't be legally employed. He had started working, illegally, in a car wash, where he was barely paid enough to buy food for himself, let alone to keep the two of us – and the baby when it was born. I wanted to work anyway. At least, I wanted to *do* something.

Things didn't work out at the mall though. It knocked my confidence when I found I couldn't cope. I had dropped out of college; the thought of going to university, or doing any other kind of higher education, was inconceivable to me; I had got the sack from the café; I hadn't coped well with a retail job … I began to wonder if I was going to be able to do any kind of legitimate work if I wasn't capable of communicating and interacting with other people. So I decided to focus on being pregnant and on trying to get my head round the prospect of becoming a full-time mother.

The problem was I didn't really know what mothers are supposed to do. Suddenly, the realisation of what was actually going to happen hit me: I was about to become responsible for another human being when I couldn't even take care of myself. Mum had always told me that having me had ruined her life. What if the child I was going to have ruined mine – even more than I had ruined it myself? What if things didn't work out with Baashir and I ended up like Mum, resentful and depressed?

I hadn't told Mum I was pregnant. I wanted to wait until I had had the first scan. But one day she opened a letter that arrived at her house – addressed to me – and went ballistic. 'What have you done?' she shouted at me. 'How could you have been so stupid?' She was even angrier when I told her I was going to have the baby and keep it. Fortunately, though, when she realised I wouldn't change my mind, however much she ranted and raved at me, she did do her best to help me.

Baashir wasn't comfortable with the idea of me living with him in the house he shared with his friends, so Mum let me go home. She even started giving me some of the Child Benefit money she got for me every week, plus money to buy food for us both, which I cooked too, thanks to the culinary skills I learned at the pupil referral unit.

Mum continued to come and go, leading the life she had established for herself during the period when our paths had rarely crossed. But after she got over the initial shock of finding out I was pregnant, we began to rebuild our relationship. It was a slow and very cautious process. The end result was never going to be perfect – too much time had passed and too many things had happened, for Mum as well as for me, I imagine. I was still angry with her too. There are always going to be aspects of the Asperger syndrome that I will struggle to deal with, but I had enough common sense and maturity by the time I was 16 to feel that, as a child, I hadn't always had the protection I should have had. Mum *was* trying though, and when I was seven months' pregnant, she even allowed Baashir to move in with us.

Within days, Mum and Baashir had become best friends. I wasn't sure how I felt about it for a while, particularly when Mum reverted to ignoring me most of the time. Then I realised that it suited me fine, because with Mum's attention taken off me, I had some space to breathe. It also meant that she was always civil to me – at least when Baashir was around: the last thing she wanted was for him to see her screaming at me and pulling my hair. So, in the end, Baashir moving in and occupying a place in Mum's affections that I had never seemed to have access to turned out to be a good thing. By taking the pressure off me, it did my relationship with Mum a power of good and gave me the peace and quiet I needed but would otherwise never have had.

The only problem was that Mum seemed to hate it if Baashir and I spent time on our own and to do everything she could think of to prevent it happening. If we were together in my bedroom, she would come storming up the stairs and bang on the door, shouting, 'Do you want a cup of tea? Are you coming downstairs? Shall I just sit down there on my own? Shall I? Is that what you want me to do?'

It only made her worse if we had tried to explain that we hadn't shut ourselves away because we hated her or didn't appreciate what she was doing for us, but because we just needed some time alone together. So we would go downstairs to sit with her in the living room, and after a while she would relax and make coquettish remarks to Baashir to make him laugh.

She reacted in a similar way whenever Baashir gave me any attention. For example, if he ever cuddled me while she was in the room, she would storm out like a spoilt, bad-tempered child having a tantrum. We got used to it in the end and when we really wanted to be on our own, we went for long walks in the countryside, then ignored Mum's sulks and the sound of slamming doors when we got home.

When I was about seven months' pregnant, I was officially considered to be no longer able to work and became entitled to Income Support. Baashir was giving me what he could spare out of his earnings at the car wash, most of which I was spending on clothes for the baby and on all the other things we were going to need after the birth. We were saving up to get married too, so I also put aside what I could for our wedding.

For a while, the wedding became almost the sole focus of my attention. The event itself was going to be a very small affair. It was really a 'visa wedding', a marriage of convenience for Baashir that would enable him to become a legitimate resident in the UK. So it was all the paperwork related to that which occupied all my time, and a considerable amount of money. Baashir's original visa – the one he had been given when he arrived in the country as a refugee at the age of 17 – had expired, which meant that, technically, he no longer lived here. And that made everything even more difficult than it would otherwise have been.

I think, at that time, when someone's visa expired they had a window of a few months to apply for a new one. During that period, their status wasn't really legal or illegal, but they had to be able to prove that they were in touch with a solicitor and making efforts to get it all sorted out. Because it was a grey area of immigration, quite a few of the people I talked to and sent forms to seemed to be as confused as I was about how it all worked and exactly what sort of proof was required.

The main problem seemed to be that without a valid visa, Baashir couldn't open a bank account, and because he was staying with me at Mum's and had no utility bills in his name, he wasn't able to prove where he was living. But without an address or any of the other paperwork he needed, he couldn't apply for permission to stay.

It took me weeks to try to sort it all out. Every day I would go to the Afghanistan Embassy in London to get forms signed, or visit other offices in other towns, talk to people on the telephone, send off photographs and all the information required by the solicitor, write letters, make more phone calls ... I became completely absorbed by it. So much so in fact that it took longer than it might otherwise have done for me to realise that while I was contributing more and more towards the cost of it all, Baashir was paying less and less.

By the time I found out that Baashir was gambling, it had already begun to dawn on me that he was earning much more at the car wash than he had led me to believe. It turned out that every week, as soon as he got paid, he was going to one of the betting shops in town and pouring money into the fruit machines. Sometimes he spent the entire day gambling and didn't go to work at all. But instead of doing something about it – confronting him at least – I ignored all the warning signs and continued to focus on trying to get his visa sorted out, which, by that time, had become almost an obsession for me.

At the same time as I was trying to sort out Baashir's visa, I was trying to get to grips with what needed to be done so that we could get married. I went to several different registry offices and spoke to the registrars, who all told me the same thing: unless Baashir had the correct visa, the wedding could not go ahead. But I refused to take no for an answer and continued to turn up almost every day on the door-steps of various offices, clutching new bits of paper-work I thought might support my case.

In the end, they got so sick of me at one registry office they palmed me off on a trainee. It was the break I had been hoping for but had begun to think was never going to come. Perhaps the trainee understood the new laws better than everyone else, or perhaps she didn't understand them at all but didn't want to say so. Whatever the reason, she signed the papers that gave Baashir the right to remain in the

UK legally for 'family reasons'. And once she had done that, we were able to get married.

Our wedding took place just over a year after we had first met. Unfortunately, however, my dogged, fixated determination to sort everything out for Baashir had taken its toll on my already precarious mental health. All I can remember about the day itself is feeling sick and panic-stricken because I didn't want to go through with it. In fact, the last coherent thought I can remember having on my wedding day is, 'I do not want to do this.'

I had started to become aware of my mental-health issues quite some time before the wedding. I have had a few counselling sessions over the last few years, but I've always been wary of talking about my problems to doctors or social workers or anyone else who might decide they need to interfere in my life. Even if they did have the best of intentions, I would be anxious in case the outcome didn't turn out to be what I would consider to be the best thing for me. So, as much as possible, I have tried to cope on my own with the various problems related to my mental health, and although I do still struggle with some of the issues, they are now mostly under control.

Even before the wedding and all the weeks leading up to it when I was trying to sort out Baashir's visa, I had begun to react to extreme stress by switching to another personality. I wasn't aware what was happening at the time. I just knew that I would sometimes get on a bus, for example, and then find myself at some unknown destination with no memory of how I had got there. It was someone else who witnessed the process and described it to me for the first time. Apparently, I suddenly went very quiet and then, after a minute or two, started talking in a different voice, using words I wouldn't normally use. The 'switch' would sometimes last for several hours. All I could remember afterwards were a few dislocated fragments of the conversations I had had, almost as if I had been really drunk.

It must have been the stress of getting married to Baashir when I knew we didn't really love each other that caused me to switch on my wedding day. I can remember what I wore – a colourful dress and a white cloak – and I know that we had dinner at a restaurant after the ceremony, then Baashir and I spent the night in a hotel before going back to Mum's the next day. But I had to look at the wedding video and photographs to find out what actually happened on the day itself.

Mum was there and so was her friend Derek from the charity shop. In fact, it was Derek who gave me away. He was very ill at the time, but he was determined to walk me down the aisle – or, at least, from the door of the registry office to the table where Baashir was waiting for me. Derek had always done what he could to help me when I was a little girl and I know he thought I would be okay with Baashir. So he was really happy to see me married before he died, a few months later.

I didn't have any understanding about my own mental health at that time. In fact, I refused to admit, even to myself, that there was anything wrong with me at all. I hadn't ever had the experience of switching while I was with Diyan. I had had rages when we were together. But even on the occasions when I wasn't able to control my anger, I had always been aware of what was happening and that it was *me* who was shouting and lashing out at him. Perhaps your mind can recognise the point at which you're under so much stress that you're about to crack, and that's when it switches *you* off, as a protective measure.

I must have been reaching that point of no return on my wedding day, and on the day my child was born a couple of months later. I don't remember anything about the birth. I know Mum and Baashir were with me, but I have no visual memory of my newborn baby or of what it felt like to hold my child for the first time. I do remember how traumatic it was afterwards, when Mum went home to have a shower and Baashir left to go and celebrate becoming a father by getting stoned and drunk with his friends. The midwives left me too, and for the next four hours I lay there in my own muck, not knowing what to do when my baby cried and wishing I had the confidence to ask for help.

It wasn't until I had left the hospital and was back at Mum's house again that the postnatal depression really set in. I still didn't ask anyone for help though. So I ended up struggling with it alone for the whole of the first year of my baby's life. It was another year of my life that is lost forever, except for just a handful of memories, most of which aren't very good ones.

During the first few weeks after the baby was born, I found a lot of things even more difficult to deal with than I had expected. One of the worst was the sleep deprivation. The baby woke up crying at least two or three times every night, and after just a few days I was totally exhausted. Sometimes, I would try to wake Baashir up, for moral support as much as anything, so that I didn't feel as though my screaming baby and I were the only people in the world who were awake. But, as well as gambling, Baashir was doing a lot of coke and becoming increasingly violent. So, instead of helping me, he would fly into a rage, kicking and strangling me, which seemed to make the baby cry even more.

I can't remember if I was consciously grateful to Mum at the time for giving us a home when she didn't have to do so. Without her help, I wouldn't have had a safe place to take my baby when I left the hospital. Clearly though, she felt that she had done enough and didn't ever offer to take the baby into her room – even for just a couple of hours so that I could get some sleep. She knew Baashir and I were having problems: it wouldn't have been possible for anyone living in the same house not to have been woken up at least sometimes by the sound of the baby crying and Baashir shouting at me. But instead of asking me what was happening or if I was okay, she asked why I was 'always winding Baashir up' and told me, often, what a really nice guy she thought he was.

As well as believing that all bad sexual experiences are the fault of the women involved, Mum believed that conception and whatever happened after it were the woman's sole responsibility too. I suppose she was right, in a way, as far as Baashir and I were concerned. It was certainly true that I had chosen to get pregnant and that no one had forced me to have the baby. But whether it had been my *fault* or not, I really needed someone's help and she was the only person I had, now that Baashir seemed to be intent on making my life even more difficult than it would otherwise have been.

When I discovered that Baashir was stealing from me to buy coke, it felt like the last straw. I was spending almost all the money I was getting in benefits on nappies and clothes for the baby. But when I started hiding it, in books and DVDs and under the mattress, he just trashed my bedroom until he found it.

I was beginning to feel overwhelmed and just wanted it all to stop. I didn't want to be with Baashir. I didn't want to have to deal with Mum's criticism of me. Perhaps most importantly of all, I didn't want my baby. Mum couldn't understand it. 'You don't even like your own kid,' she would say angrily. 'You can't even be a decent parent.' I was too weary and depressed to even think to remind her that, for as long as I could remember, I had grown up with the knowledge that *she* hadn't ever wanted *me*.

Despite everything though, I did take care of my baby's physical needs during that first year, when I was struggling to cope. I was breast-feeding for the first six months, so at least the baby was always fed, even when Baashir stole my money and I couldn't buy food for myself. Mum was reluctant to help me financially, which was reasonable enough in view of the fact that I was getting Income Support and living in her house. But even when I told her that Baashir was stealing from me, she just shrugged and didn't answer.

In the end, I was so sleep deprived I barely knew what I was doing; so hungry and malnourished I sometimes collapsed; and so guilty about the fact that I didn't love my child my self-esteem had sunk to an all-time low. It was horrible. Everything was horrible. Although I seemed to be surrounded by people, I didn't have anyone to turn to for help. I didn't tell the health visitor about any of my problems because I was afraid of social services becoming involved. Fortunately, she was as easily fooled by clean clothes and a well-fed baby as the social workers had been when I was a child. I don't know what she would have thought if she had known I was nicking nappies and baby clothes from Asda.

Chapter 13

I knew by the time my baby was just a few weeks old that the life Baashir used to describe to me when we sat together in his bed had just been a dream. There wasn't going to be a shop with a flat above it where we would raise our children and be a family. The reality was that he didn't want to be a husband or a father. In fact, he didn't want to have anything to do with our child, and as the months went by, we often didn't see him for days on end. At least when he stayed away, he wasn't stealing my money.

Again, Mum seemed to blame me for all of it – for getting pregnant, for not being able to love my baby, for 'driving Baashir away'. Her attitude was, 'You've made your bed, now lie in it'. And that *was* what I was trying to do. It was just that, however hard I tried,

I didn't seem to be able to stop myself sinking into a state of depression.

Then, when my baby was six months old, the Income Support payments stopped and I was put on Jobseeker's Allowance. Because we were married and Baashir was still waiting for his visa to come through, so couldn't work or claim benefits, I was considered to be the breadwinner, while he was expected, reasonably enough, to be a stay-at-home dad. He *was* working in fact, still at the car wash. But because it wasn't legitimate work, the pay was really poor, probably barely enough to buy food for him to eat once he had fed his gambling and coke habits.

I sometimes stood outside the gates of the car wash waiting for Baashir to finish his shift so that I could ask him for money. But usually he refused and it was one of his friends who gave me a few pounds to buy nappies and clothes for my child.

For the first year after my baby was born, I woke up every single morning wishing I was somewhere else, living someone else's life. I was under so much stress that I don't remember very much about those months, which means that I don't have any of the precious memories most parents have – of hearing their child's first word and watching them take their first steps. Gradually though, as my baby became a toddler, there were mornings when I would wake up with a sense that something was different, and then realise that I didn't have the terrible feeling of dread I had become so used to. I began to become aware of smells too – the warm-milk-and-soap smell of my child, for example, or the almost tangible odour of cut grass.

For months, I had been forcing myself to get through 'just one day', and then another, because I didn't seem to have any alternative. As I began to emerge from the fog of depression, I started to think about the future and about what job I might be able to do to earn some money and build an independent life for myself and my child.

When I signed on at the Jobcentre, the only jobs that seemed to be available involved working a 40-hour week. I asked Mum and Baashir if they would look after my child while I was at work, but when they both refused, I had to turn down all the job interviews I was offered. So then they stopped my money: refusing to go for interviews meant that I wasn't seeking a job, and therefore I wasn't entitled to receive Jobseeker's Allowance. I wasn't eligible for financial help with day care either, because, technically, I had a childcare provider in Baashir. When the Jobseeker's Allowance stopped, all I had to survive on was £20 a week Child Benefit plus the money Mum's cousin Cora sometimes gave me.

Every time one thing got better, something else seemed to get worse. Then something happened that changed everything – or, at least, brought the future into some sort of focus so that it began to seem as though things did have a point and a purpose after all: I began to love my child.

One apparently insurmountable problem still remained, however. As I had only a very basic education and no qualifications, I wasn't going to be able to find a job that would pay enough for me to put my child in day care. And if I couldn't work, I couldn't pull us out of the situation we were in and create a good future for us both. Once again, I felt as though I was trapped in a vicious circle that threatened to pitch me straight back into the hopeless, helpless state I thought I was just beginning to emerge from.

When you feel as though you haven't got anything left to lose, you do things you might not otherwise have done. For me, that happened on one of the many days when I had run out of money. Except that on this particular day I realised that nothing was going to change unless I did something to change it. So I strapped my child into the buggy, walked to

Diyan's flat, rang the doorbell and when he opened the door, said simply, 'I need some nappies.'

Sometimes, it's just a case of looking for help in the right places, which aren't necessarily the most obvious ones. But I knew Diyan would help me. He took us to the supermarket that day and bought some of the things I needed. Then we went back to his flat and he made a meal for us all.

Apparently, things hadn't been going well between Diyan and his wife. He had made a couple of journeys to Iran to see her during the previous 12 months, but they had argued incessantly when he was there, and after his second visit he had decided not to bring her over to this country after all. 'I *really* regret my marriage,' he told me. 'I haven't been able to stop thinking about the mistake I made.'

We started seeing each other again after that. We didn't sleep together though. We had gone through too much to be able to fall in love again. But I did still love him. Fortunately for me and my child, he must have still loved me too. And although I felt sad because I knew we couldn't ever have the sort of relationship we had had before, I was very grateful to have a friend, particularly one like Diyan. As well as buying nappies for my child, he cooked meals for us and put a seat in the back of his car so that he could take us to the beach for days out. It wasn't the family I had dreamed of having, but it was infinitely better than the reality I had become used to.

My mental health had already started to improve before the day I knocked on Diyan's door. I don't think I would have had the confidence to ask for his help otherwise, or to accept it without feeling that I had to sleep with him, even though he didn't ever put any pressure on me himself. Over the next few weeks, with his support, the improvement continued and eventually I began to send out emails looking for work.

I didn't dare to believe that, this time, maybe something would get better without something else getting worse. But it did start to look that way when I was offered an apprenticeship working as a teaching assistant in a junior school. It was only for a couple of days a week, but it wouldn't have been possible at all if Mum hadn't changed her mind and agreed to look after her grandchild for the two mornings if I paid for day care in the afternoons. At first, I didn't think that was going to be feasible, as I was 19 and would be earning an apprentice wage of just £2.65 an hour. But when it turned out that I would also be entitled to tax credits, I knew that I could make it work.

After 14 months of rummaging through the 20p bucket at the charity shop, I can still remember how I felt the first time I went into Mothercare and bought a brand new top for my child. A few weeks later, I was a working mum with childcare in place and, potentially, a future that held opportunities for us both. With Diyan's support – and then Mum's too – I had gained enough self-confidence to break the vicious circle. The one thing that hadn't improved was my relationship with Baashir.

Although Baashir spent most of his time elsewhere, he did come to Mum's sometimes. But he still showed absolutely no interest in our child and was becoming increasingly violent towards me, often pushing me around and hitting me. Eventually, things came to a head one night when we invited a friend of his for dinner, with his wife and young son.

The little boy was quite badly behaved, although neither of his parents seemed to notice, and the wife was very quiet. I had seen her husband hit her on a previous occasion and it was obvious that she was frightened of him. In the end, I got fed up with sitting there watching Baashir and his friend get more and more drunk while the little boy trashed Mum's house. So I asked the man to leave. It was late and I was tired, but I should have anticipated Baashir's reaction. He was furious with me for embarrassing him in front of his friend and we started arguing. Then his friend hit his wife for failing to control their son, and Baashir hit me.

The next thought I had was so clear and definite it was almost as though I had actually heard a voice in my head saying, 'I am not taking this anymore'. And then I hit Baashir back. It's surprising what impact 5 feet 3 inches of outraged indignation can have on 6 feet of shocked embarrassment. Baashir never hit me again after that day. He tried a few times, but soon backed off when I retaliated – with a frying pan on the first occasion and by almost pushing him through one of the plasterboard walls of Mum's rented house on the second. Finally, though, he got the message that I had had enough.

For the first 19 years of my life, I had been just like Baashir's friend's wife – bullied and intimidated into doing whatever someone else told me to do. In my case though, it wasn't just one person who I had allowed to coerce and abuse me. Because I hated myself and didn't have any self-esteem or confidence, I wasn't ever surprised when other people seemed to hate me too. So I never fought back when they treated me badly, and I never said 'No'. Now though, it was as if something previously dormant inside my head had been sparked into life and I had had enough of being pushed around.

It was Diyan who gave me the confidence to work, and it was working – and perhaps also becoming a parent – that gave me the confidence to stand up for myself at last. Baashir was a bully and, like most bullies, he thought twice about hitting someone who was going to fight back. And what I lacked in stature was more than made up for by the anger and frustration that had been building up inside me for years.

Baashir was still trying to steal my money, by taking it out of my bank account when he didn't have access to my cash. Once I had decided that I was no longer going to be intimidated by him, I changed my PIN and, this time, stood my ground when he threatened me and refused to tell him what it was.

He kept coming to Mum's house, staying for a few days and then disappearing again. But it wasn't anything he did – at least, not directly – that finally prompted me to end our relationship for good. It was an incident that occurred at day care when our child was two years old and apparently attacked and tried to strangle a little boy.

'I'm really sorry,' I told the nursery teacher. 'I don't know why it happened.' Which wasn't true:

I knew exactly why it had happened. It was because our child had often witnessed Baashir doing the same thing to me. It was the wake-up call I needed and when I got home that day I asked Baashir to leave.

It was several months before he finally stopped climbing in through a window or hiding in the garden. Sometimes, I would be watching television and would glance up and see him standing there in the dark, just looking at me. When I went into town, he often followed me around, like some creepy stalker. He was taking a lot of coke by that time, so I think his brain was pretty much scrambled and he didn't really know what he was doing.

He didn't ever seem to want to speak to me when he saw me in town. But, one day, he suddenly grabbed me by the throat and started bashing my head against a wall. I might have let even that pass if he hadn't then snatched up our child and told me, 'I would rather kill us both than allow my child to live with a woman like you.' That was breaking point for me. Even now, I may sometimes be slow to protect myself, but the one thing I will not put up with under any circumstances is someone frightening or threatening to hurt my child. So I called the police.

After I had given my statement to the police, a woman from social services came to the house and said, 'If you've got domestic violence issues, we will have to seriously consider whether we need to take your child into care.' She looked at me with an expression that seemed to suggest she thought domestic violence was both shameful and entirely avoidable – like bedbugs or the infestation of cockroaches I think she expected to find during her inspection of the house.

First, she checked the kitchen, opening cupboard doors and running her hands over every surface, presumably looking for dirt or dust that, in Mum's house, wouldn't ever have been allowed to settle. Then she came into the living room, and I watched in silence while she lifted up the cushions one by one and examined the spotless white sofa. Afterwards, when she was about to leave and was standing by the front door, clutching her clipboard, she told me, 'If you allow him to come here again, we will view it as a failure to protect your child, who will then be placed under a temporary care order while you consider your options.'

I was angry because she seemed to believe that I *wanted* Baashir to be around, when it was because I had told him to leave that the trouble had started in the first place. It seemed unfair, too, that after I had gone to the police because of the threats Baashir had made, she was treating me as though I was the one putting my child at risk.

I had already made my choice between my husband and my child. In reality, there hadn't ever been any choice to make. But at least what the social worker said focused my mind on the fact that there was far more at stake than my own well-being if Baashir ever managed to force or trick his way into the house again.

I dropped the case against him after the social worker's visit though, because I knew that just the possibility of the police becoming involved would be enough to keep him away. And I was right, because when he did approach me in the street a couple of times after that, he soon backed off when I got out my phone and threatened to call them again.

Reporting Baashir to the police was another turning point for me. It felt as if, after eight years of being chased by bullies and abusers, I had finally stopped running away and had turned to face them. I suppose I should have known Mum wouldn't see things quite the same way. She was furious with me for going to the police, not least because, in her eyes, it wasn't Baashir who was to blame for anything that had happened, not even for stealing from me and being physically violent. 'He was such a nice young man when you met him,' she told me. 'What have you done to him? It's your fault he's changed. You pushed him to it. Just look at what you drive people to do.'

So now I had social services on my back, Baashir wanting to beat the crap out of me and Mum accusing me of being a terrible person. It was like being in some surreal nightmare, surrounded by the contorted faces of people who were pointing their fingers at me and saying, 'You're doing a bad job. You're a bad wife, a bad daughter, a bad mother.' In fact though, once social services had established that my child was living somewhere clean and that there were going to be no more complaints of domestic violence, they didn't bother about us again.

That left me with just Diyan on my side. I wouldn't have had anyone at all if I hadn't had him. Things were hard, but they had been harder. I was determined to carry on with my job and get some sort of qualification, because I knew that was the only way I was going to be able to pull myself up and out of the situation I was in. If I was earning some money, I would be able to focus all my efforts on building a life for myself and my child.

* * *

Diyan continued to be my only friend until about five or six months after I had kicked Baashir out for the last time, when I started seeing an English guy called Wyatt. It was the first 'normal' adult relationship I had ever had, and the first time I had fallen head over heels in love. Unfortunately, however, it seemed that, for me, falling in love with someone normal and decent was as stressful as being used and abused by a man who just wanted a visa and didn't really love me at all. And as soon as I was subjected to any kind of stress, my mental health began to suffer.

It was as if there was a horrible, malevolent goblin sitting on my shoulder, whispering crazy things in my ear, telling me I didn't deserve the good thing that was happening to me. And eventually, as the goblin's voice grew louder, I started lashing out at Wyatt, just like I had done with Diyan.

Only a few people have ever seen me switch. It's something I'm very ashamed of, even though I know I don't have any control over it, and I had no under-standing of what was happening at the time. Recently, someone who has witnessed it explained it to me by saying, 'It's like watching that film *The Exorcist*. Suddenly, your eyes roll back into your head. Then you clench your jaws, grind your teeth and start to shake. When you speak again, your voice sounds completely different. In fact, you become a completely different, and quite aggressive, person.'

I know I switched a few times when I was seeing Wyatt. Even though he must have been very shocked by it, he stayed with me for two or three months and really did try to help and support me. But you couldn't expect anyone to put up with something like for very long. I was devastated when it all went wrong. He was a really nice guy, with a good job, earning good money, and he treated me the way I had always imagined a decent man would treat someone he cared about. I hated myself when he left me. And I hated the goblin on my shoulder that controlled my mental health.

The one thing I am very grateful about is the fact that my postnatal depression was at its worst when my child was just a baby and so wasn't aware of, or doesn't remember, what I was like. I had always been wary of talking about my problems to anyone, particularly to someone who might be in a position to get social services involved, because my main fear was that they would take my child away. But as soon as I realised I was starting to get a bit better – which was some time before I met Wyatt – I had some counselling, because I was terrified of slipping back into depression.

It was my doctor who arranged for me to see the counsellor, and it was the counsellor who explained to me that what I had experienced from the age of 11 was actually abuse. Until then, I had believed that what had happened was all my fault. She was a good counsellor in many ways, but she didn't have any experience of dealing with child abuse, so I probably ended up with more problems than I had had when I first started talking to her.

I was still coping with life during the time when I was seeing her. I had survived the first couple of years of being a mother – and, more importantly, so had my child; I had survived Baashir; and I had survived all the horrible, abusive years of my childhood. So it seemed particularly ironic that after everything I *had* survived, it began to look as though falling in love might be the thing that was finally going to defeat me.

I think, in general, it's the stress of trying to conceal the fact that there's anything wrong with me that tips the balance of my mental health. It was certainly my fear of Wyatt finding out who I really was that caused me to self-harm for the first time – if you don't count self-harming by proxy, which is what I was really doing during the time when I was being used and abused by Saleem and his friends.

I was self-harming – cutting myself – throughout the time I was with Wyatt. I used the serrated blade of a kitchen knife on the first occasion. I can remember watching the red line of blood that appeared on my arm as I ran the tip of the blade across my skin. In fact, I was so mesmerised by the blood that seeped out of the cut that I didn't feel the pain to begin with. Afterwards though, as the wound began to heal, I was repulsed by how ugly it looked. So the next time I cut my thigh.

I didn't ever cut myself in front of Wyatt, of course. But I did sometimes dig my nails into the back of my hand until it bled, to try to anchor myself to reality when I realised I was about to switch. It didn't work though. It seemed that the harder I tried to stop myself switching, the more stressed I became; and the more stressed I became, the more I switched.

I hated the sensation I had when it was about to happen. It was like standing on the edge of a very steep cliff and feeling myself start to fall backwards. That was the point at which I would dig my nails into my hand. Sometimes it prolonged the moment when I was teetering on the precipice. But I always fell in the end – although, oddly, my feet remained anchored to the ground, so that it was just my body that dropped like a stone towards some unseen surface below me.

I had desperately wanted to hide from Wyatt the fact that I wasn't 'normal'. But the stress of falling in love with him made my mental-health problems worse and, ultimately, I couldn't blame him for breaking things off. After he left me, everything fell apart. So I did what I always did when I couldn't cope anymore and started drinking heavily.

I had a friend called Lyn, who I loved to bits but who was a serious drinker. She used to drink at one of the local parks with a group of African guys, and when Wyatt and I split up, I started going down there with her – and taking my child, who was about two years old. I wasn't sleeping with anyone, so I thought it was all fine and that I was actually keeping my child safe. In reality, of course, I put both of us in some potentially dangerous situations, which I'm incredibly ashamed of now. Fortunately, Lyn's friends were very protective of us. I don't even dare think about what might have happened if they hadn't looked out for us the way they did.

I can't believe I actually thought that getting drunk while in charge of a child was okay on any level, but especially after what I had experienced myself when I was about the same age and lived in Cora's flat with Mum and the assortment of alco-holic, drug-addicted oddballs who were her friends.

I thought I was a good mother because my child was always well fed and wearing clean clothes – and loved, after the first year. But that was exactly what my mum had thought about her parenting skills during my dysfunctional childhood. And I knew that she was wrong.

I can't even begin to understand why I didn't see the similarities between her weed smoking and my drinking, or between the excuses we made to ourselves so that we could continue to do what we wanted to do while telling ourselves that we were doing okay as parents. The truth is, it was only by pure luck that I managed to keep my child safe – and perhaps, to some extent, because I was aware in a way my mum hadn't been of the dangers that children need to be protected from.

I thought my child was happy playing with toys in the park, eating the sandwiches I always took with me and then being wrapped in a coat and settled down for a sleep on my lap. I was quite proud of the fact that, no matter how drunk I was, I could always change a nappy. I would sit there late into the night, with this little sleeping bundle on my knee, drinking and laughing with my new friends. I actually did think that I was doing a good job. Whereas, in reality, it was neglect, pure and simple. History was repeating itself. I cannot believe now that I didn't see that at the time.

After Wyatt left me, my greatest fear was that my mental health might deteriorate to the point at which I might harm my child. I know that sounds like an excuse, but it was one of the main reasons why I went to the park every day, because the only time I felt happy and believed that everything was under control was when I was drinking in the company of other people.

I had wanted to have friends for as long as I could remember. But, despite my best efforts, I hadn't ever managed to make any, either at school or when I hung around with the guys who groomed and abused me. So being accepted by Lyn and her friends and included in their group, rather than being merely tolerated or exploited, was a new experience for me.

As long as my mental health was under control, I wasn't going to throw myself off a bridge or in front of a train. So I thought it was better for my child too. And maybe it was better than having the burden of your mother's suicide hanging over you like a sword for the rest of your life, or wondering why she didn't love you enough to stay with you and look after you while you were growing up.

I Know What You Are

I think I will always feel guilty about some of the things I did during the first two or three years of my child's life, even though I tell myself now that I was doing the best I could at the time. Most of all I hate the thought that I was repeating the mistakes my mum had made with me. There is one very important difference between my own childhood and that of my child, however, because I didn't ever know that I was loved.

Chapter 14

I hung out with Lyn and her friends for about a year. It was company I needed more than alcohol. So although I did get drunk, I probably wasn't drinking as much when I was with people at the park as I might have done if I had been sitting on my own at home. Although if I had stayed at home, of course, my child would at least have been asleep in a bed.

One day, we went to the park in the afternoon and I woke up back at home in my own bed with no memory of how I had got there. My first, panicked, thought was for my child, who I found in the kitchen sitting on the floor by the open fridge door surrounded by yoghurt pots and spilt milk, trying to find something to eat.

Because of the Asperger syndrome, I am not always aware of all the potential dangers that are apparent to other people. So I had always known that I was going to have to try even harder than other parents do to keep my child safe. Getting so drunk that night that I had no idea where I had been or what I had done, then falling into a catatonic stupor while my child scavenged for food could not, by any stretch of the imagination, be seen as 'doing my best'.

From my early teens, I had used alcohol whenever I needed to be able to blur reality and separate myself from whatever traumatic events I was going through at the time. Most recently, I had used it to dull the heartache of losing Wyatt. I had often risked my own life during the past six or seven years, but suddenly I actually *understood* that it wasn't just my life I was risking now. I was shocked and ashamed by what I had allowed to happen and since that night I have never had a drink when I was with my child and have only been drunk a handful of times.

It wasn't until I stopped getting drunk every day that I realised alcohol and depression had been affecting other areas of my life too. I had already been given an ultimatum at work: 'Either pull yourself together and admit you need some help or we don't want you here anymore.' And although I didn't take their advice about asking for any help, I did manage to hold things together while I finished the apprenticeship, and then got a place at college to do an access to higher education course.

Without the masking effects of alcohol, however, the goblin on my shoulder started shouting so loudly I was struggling to cope. Even though my heart gradually mended itself, I felt I had failed with Wyatt and that I wasn't ever going to be capable of having a normal relationship. With alcohol off the menu, I turned to the only other mind-numbing, self-destructive activity I was familiar with and started sleeping around with men I met on dating websites.

My justification for what I was doing was that seeing men without getting close to any of them was a way of taking my mind off everything else and stabilising my mental health. It was an irrational excuse, of course, not only because meeting up with men I didn't know to have sex was intrinsically unsafe, but also because it didn't have a very positive effect on my confidence, self-esteem or, ultimately, mental health. Somehow though, it seemed to keep me from sinking any deeper into hopeless depression, although I was balanced very precariously on the edge.

Mum still went out a lot, and on a couple of occasions when she wasn't in, I invited men I didn't know to the house. Again, like drinking at the park, I don't know why I thought that was okay, or why I didn't realise that I was risking both my own safety and that of my child, who was asleep in bed upstairs. I think I focused on alcohol as being the only real problem, and as I wasn't drinking during the day or at any other time when my child was awake and in my sole care, anything else seemed to be all right.

I did get very drunk on a few occasions, but only as a last resort when I was on the verge of being over-whelmed by depression and anxiety. I told myself it didn't matter if it was only once in a while. Each time it happened, I made a solemn promise to myself the next morning that it had been the last time. Then I didn't drink again for at least a couple of weeks, until something happened to make me feel as though everything was spinning out of control again.

Things did change in September, when I started college. I couldn't go on forever pretending that the drinking was a form of self-medicating that wasn't doing any real damage. Despite all the problems I had – because of the autism and because of the abuse I had suffered as a child – I *knew* I could do some-thing better with my life. All I had to do was work out what. But to be able to do that, I first had to wean myself off my addiction to alcohol – because it *was* an addiction, whether or not I was prepared to admit it.

What helped in the end was the fact that I loved college.

It was incredibly stressful for the first few weeks, meeting new people and not knowing how to behave or what I was supposed to be doing. In fact, I had a few problems initially, including some mental-health flare-ups and several incidents of switching. And I started self-harming again too. Then I began to find myself having conversations with people and realising that they were laughing at something I had said and being genuinely friendly. It was a huge surprise to me to discover that I was actually capable of living in the normal world, being a college student and making friends.

When I completed the access course at college, I got a place at university, which I ended up delaying for a year, so that my child would be at nursery full time and I would have had a whole year more to continue getting better. It also meant that the divorce Baashir refused to give me when I asked him would have come through automatically, as we'd have been separated for two years. I was very happy at college, so I'm really looking forward to going to university.

* * *

Since I was diagnosed with Asperger syndrome almost 15 years ago, I've learned to deal with quite a lot of its aspects. I still walk into danger sometimes, because I don't see the warning signs that are probably easily apparent to most other people. And I've still got lots of issues that make relationships difficult for me – as well as for the poor men who get involved with me.

It's as if there's an aberration that has been hard-wired into the depths of my psyche so that I believe that the only proof of my existence is the attention someone else is paying to me, usually some man I don't really know and who doesn't even matter to me. I'm going to keep fighting it though, and maybe eventually all the 'bad' neural networks in my brain will reorganise themselves and I'll be normal at last! I know that won't ever be quite true, because you can't cure Asperger syndrome. But, if you're lucky like I am, you can learn to cope with it well enough to be able to make real friends, so that you won't have to be alone for the rest of your life.

I know that the time has come for me to stop trying to manage my mental health on my own and get some professional help. I probably should have done it some time ago. But I'm still afraid to ask for the assistance I need, because if social services find out that I have mental-health problems, they might take my child away. And I honestly don't think that would be the best thing for my child – or for me.

The last time I decided that I *had* to get help was more than a year ago now. I went to an NHS drop-in centre, quite late in the day, and had already signed in when the anxiety made me switch. It usually only lasts an hour or two these days; then I pull myself back. This time though, without being conscious of what I was doing, I walked out of the drop-in centre and down to the river. When I eventually came to, I had one leg over the barrier and some man who had been fishing had his arm around my waist, trying to stop me climbing over and dropping down into the river below.

It upset me so much I decided I wouldn't ever try to get help again. But I've got a friend who says that I must and that he'll go with me next time, so that I'm not alone if the fear takes over. He's someone I can trust – without him and Diyan, I'm pretty sure I wouldn't still be here today – and he's every bit as determined by nature as I am. So it will be interesting to see what happens.

I'm in a good place at the moment. I'm taking care of my child and getting on reasonably well with my mum. I haven't had a switching episode for more than four months, and I haven't self-harmed or been drunk for even longer. It's because things are going so well that I'm even more reluctant than usual to start getting involved with doctors or social workers or anyone else who might end up making everything worse rather than better.

Part of moving forward with my life has meant closing the chapter of it that involved Diyan, which is sad, although inevitable, I suppose. He did bring his wife over to this country in the end, but he was very unhappy. In fact, the last time I saw him, a few months ago, he was very depressed and almost in tears as he told me about the problems they have been having. I felt really sorry for him, and really bad for not wanting to get drawn into it all in case it dragged me back into a world I know I have to leave behind me, in the past.

That makes me sound horrible, after everything Diyan has done for me. I wouldn't be going to university at all if it hadn't been for him insisting on my phoning the social worker that time to tell her I had changed my mind and did want to go to the pupil referral unit after all. But I *have* to look after myself now, because if I can't take care of myself, how can I possibly take care of my child? That's my priority and I daren't risk getting dragged down by something

I have a choice about. Apart from anything else, I have to accept the possibility that just one more worry might prove to be the one that tips the balance of my mental health.

My child and I have moved out of Mum's house for similar reasons really. It took me a long time to realise that what happened to me when I was a very young child wasn't my fault. I do have a type of autism and I know that made me more 'difficult' to deal with than a child who doesn't have it. But I *was* a child, and I often only reacted the way I did because I was frightened and confused by things that other people understand and take for granted.

I know Mum has her own mental-health issues to deal with, but I think she was wrong to blame me for whatever it was that made life such a struggle for her. Even more importantly, she shouldn't have told me when I was a child that I was responsible for her unhappiness. I think she has always believed that having a child not only ruined her life but also made her weaker. Whereas I have had completely the opposite experience: having a child has given me a purpose and strength I didn't have before.

Some of my mental-health issues – the mood swings and tendency to become depressed – might be hereditary and some might be the result of what happened to me when I was a child. Whatever the causes might be, it's because I want to break the family tradition of not talking about things that matter that I don't try to hide my bad days from my child. Above all, I want to make sure that *my* child doesn't grow up feeling guilty about *my* problems.

I know my mum didn't set out with the intention of causing me psychological damage. I'm sure she didn't for a moment realise what she was doing, or that it was because I wasn't protected and didn't have any sense of self-worth that I was such an easy victim for the men who abused and exploited me. But it was because I want to be the best mother I can possibly be that my child and I recently moved out of Mum's house and into a flat, which we share with a couple of my girlfriends.

As well as signing off on my relationship with Mum, both mentally and emotionally, I'm staying away from men too, for the time being. It's a bit lonely sometimes, and I still wish I could have a proper relationship with a decent man. But I know from experience that being with someone I care about is possibly the most significant trigger for my mental health. And when it's a choice between being with someone or being sane enough to look after my child, there really is no choice.

The problem is that whenever I find someone I think I could potentially fall in love with, the stress makes me switch. So they either meet the bolshie, confident, fun-loving 'switched-on' me first and then don't like the quieter, more reserved 'real me' when I resurface. Or they can't cope with my mood swings, which result from the stress of wanting it all to work out well but being afraid that it won't; so they don't hang around long enough to find out who I really am.

There have been many times over the last few years when I would have liked to have been able to ask social services for help. The reason I haven't done so recently is because of what the social worker said about taking my child away after I made a complaint about domestic violence. So I am doing the best I can to repair myself.

If I didn't have my child, I don't think there would be any point to any of it. It's the only reason I've clung on during all the times when it would have been much easier simply to walk into the river or go to sleep and never have to wake up again. But whenever I have thought about taking the 'easy' way out, I've imagined my child asking, 'Why did my mummy leave me?' And that's a question no one should ever have to ask.

I grew up feeling alone and unloved and, perhaps even worse, unworthy of being loved. In fact, throughout my entire childhood I felt grateful to my mum whenever she spent any time with me, because I believed that I was a horrible child. So I know what that does to the place deep inside you where bad things get stored away until they become an indestructible part of your self-image.

I have a friend who often tells me that none of what happened to me in my childhood was my fault. He says that I should feel good about the fact that I have been strong enough to pull myself through it without any help. Sometimes though, when you are used to believing that you're only responsible for the bad things, it's hard to accept it when someone says something positive about you.

I think that if you tell a child something often enough from a young enough age, there will always be a part of their brain that believes it, even when they're old enough to understand all the reasons why it isn't true. So although I *know* that it wasn't my fault that I was abused when I was a child, or that I have Asperger syndrome, or that Mum's life was so difficult, there's still a part of me that can't quite accept that I'm not to blame, for some of it at least.

I don't know if the day will ever come when I forgive myself for what happened to me and re-evaluate my self-worth, but I hope that it will. For now though, I'm just happy that my life is finally worth living, thanks to the child I love.

Poems

by Taylor Edison

The guy in the car

I dont like you
I really dont
Surely you see
The disgust as I turn away
My muscles tighten
My belly hardens
As you invade
Back pressed in the clutch
Cry out
Tears sliding down my soul
Red hot
Deep inside
A groan
A grunt

Taylor Edison and Jane Smith

All done
You pass me a tissue
Dont say a word
Its burning
Sore and bruised
I shift
I wiggle
Swallow the pain
My skin itches
Long to be clean
You never even said please
Others shake their heads
Give me a long hard stare
They dont care
The disgust crawls across their face
As I turn up in your car
Push me
Shove me into the back seat
Another man
More hands
Everywhere
Clutch my bottle
Hold it close
Seek comfort
From the smooth cold glass

Tentative footsteps

Leather seats
Felt good
On a high
Maybe its the weed
That fills the car
Going out on a date
Picked my clothes
The night before
Wanted to look all grownup
Padded bras
Tight jeans
Thought you liked me
Thought you meant it when you said
I was hot
It went too fast
Didnt think nothing of it
As you fumbled with your flies
Driving
Driving
Your hand in my hair
The smell
Cheesy and sick
The taste

Taylor Edison and Jane Smith

The texture
Of you deep in my mouth
A bus
Hear the engines
Could have died
As you laughed
At everyone sharing my shame
Girls going to school
Looking at my shame
I knew
I was dirty
Disgusting and sick

Cartoon pants

I dont know you
Dont know your name
But I know what pants you wear
If I see you in town
You walk on by
Never once look at my face
Never once looked at my face
I know your secret
As you smile and laugh with your mates
Hold hands and push the trolley with your missus
I know you
What you are
I know the sounds you make
As you grasp me from behind
Your name dont matter
I seen more
I know the face
Twisted and angry
I know the voice
Sneering and cruel
You keep especially for me
What would your wife say
If she knew

Taylor Edison and Jane Smith

How you got your kicks
Out of a twelve year old?
Asking if she were sore
Laughing at how she winced
Tender and Torn

*A bad girl**

A bad girl
Dirty and uninvited
Wrestle on the back seat
Hair pulled, pinned down
This is love
The way I know it
Turns my stomach
Knowing I never felt a touch
Without my mind flying far
Dirty sex doesnt hurt me
Wham bam thank you ma'am
Yet kisses and gentle touch
I'm not here
Feel the pleasure
And that is all
Shut my eyes
I'm not here
Feel the pleasure and nothing in my heart
Love flying free
Mind empty
You make me feel alive

* Written when I had my first good relationship.

Taylor Edison and Jane Smith

My mind so sensitive to your touch
Bring me back baby
Make me feel alive

This love is not mine

This love is not mine
No longer close enough to hurt
They hide in the back of my mind
Tainting my thoughts
The love I have now is beautiful
Yet voices whisper in my mind
Saying it won't last
I don't deserve it
Close my eyes
And see faces, leering and dark
How they laugh when they see me dare
Shrug off the memories
And try to start afresh
Every good thought
They spring attack dragging my dreams
Back into the dark
Voices whisper in my mind
I don't deserve this
I'll never be happy
I belong to them
In more ways than I'll ever admit
This battle between me and my demons
Drains me

They want me down with them, low enough for
    them to pounce
Leave me shaking and sick
With memories that should have been forgot
How they hate that you can fight them for me
They hate the blossoms of hope
You plant in my mind
Hate that you make me love myself
My mind is crippled when you say I am beautiful
Dare I believe these words?
A battle in my mind
To leave behind everything I know
To learn how to love
And how love should be received
Patience with me my darling
I am fighting an army inside my mind that's hell
    bent on my own destruction

About the Author

Taylor Edison knows that the ghosts from her childhood will never magically disappear, but the fact that she has learned to live in peace with them has at least stripped them of the power they had to haunt her.

For Taylor, it was education that enabled her to escape from her past, and in September 2016, she attained a goal she once thought would always be beyond her reach, when she started university. When she graduates, she plans to put her degree and her own experiences to good use by working with children who have even less than she had when she was a child.

Jane Smith is the ghostwriter of numerous bestselling books, including several *Sunday Times* top ten bestsellers. www.janesmithghostwriter.com

Moving Memoirs

Stories of hope, courage and the power of love…

If you loved this book, then you will love our Moving Memoirs eNewsletter

Sign up to…

- Be the first to hear about new books

- Get sneak previews from your favourite authors

- Read exclusive interviews

- Be entered into our monthly prize draw to win one of our latest releases before it's even hit the shops!

Sign up at

www.moving-memoirs.com